WHERE IS GOD WHEN A CHILD SUFFERS?

WHERE IS GOD WHEN A CHILD SUFFERS?

By

Penny Rosell Giesbrecht

Foreword by Ross Campbell, M.D., Author of
How to Really Love Your Child and many other books

Hannibal Books
Hannibal, Missouri—"America's Home Town"

(Use coupon in back to order extra copies of this and other helpful books.)

Dedicated to Jeremy
and the cousins he'll talk with in heaven someday:
Tommy Greene
Pammy Woodworth
Nancy Hultstrand
Norman Hultstrand

Contents

Foreword by Ross Campbell, M.D.   9

1   "Chosen by Jehovah"   11
2   "Please Don't Take My Baby"   21
3   "Something's Wrong With Jeremy"   31
4   No Answers   39
5   The "Angel" Escaped   49
6   Autistic?   57
7   The Healing Service   67
8   "Jeremy's on Fire!"   77
9   "It's Not Your Fault"   87
10   The Bond of Suffering   97
11   "Dear God, Where Are You?"   109
12   A Gift of Love   117
13   "God With Us"   125
14   ". . . Going Home at Last"   135
15   "Mommy, I Stepped on God!"   147
16   When a Child Suffers   153

Epilogue   163
Acknowledgements   171

Foreword

by
Ross Campbell, M.D.

Author of *How to Really Love Your Child, How to Really Love Your Teenager, How to Really Know Your Child* and other best selling parenting books.

Every five or ten years a really good book comes along on suffering. C.S. Lewis' *The Problem of Pain* and Philip Yancey's *Where Is God When It Hurts?* are classics. Penny Giesbrecht's *Where Is God When a Child Suffers?* is the book for now. It's even better, especially for a family, than the other two because it's so experiential. You learn as you walk with the Giesbrecht family in their pain.

I painfully identified with Penny and Tim as they agonized with their child. Oh, how I wish there had been a book like this when my wife, Pat, and I were suffering with our daughter Kathy. When we couldn't understand. A book to help us resolve the questions which were so troubling.

We got all the easy answers and none of them helped. I went to a pastor for counsel. All he gave me was, "Everybody's blaming God. Don't you blame Him." That was it. I went looking for Christian biographies, thinking I would get help from what others had gone through. Was that a joke. I was left feeling that other Christians didn't have the same problems and questions that Pat and I had. I only felt worse. I was the odd ball. There must be something wrong with me and my faith for feeling the way I did. I know now that the Christian biographies I read were dishonest. They put in the good and left out the bad.

The biographies may be a little better today, but we still want a quick and simple explanation for our suffering. As on television, we like to think every problem in life can be handled in 30 minutes. Or that we can pick up a solution like a hamburger at a fast food window. As a husband, father, and psychiatrist, I can tell you that life isn't like that.

Nor is the story of the Giesbrecht family. Penny is brutally honest in telling their story. Here are two wonderful, Christ-loving, Bible-believing Christian parents faced with some of the most awesome problems about life. They agonize. They cry. They get angry. They question God. And through it all they learn more things about themselves and the love of God than most people ever grasp.

How Penny "wraps up" the book and puts things together is really outstanding. Not that she puts everything in a pigeon hole, because the Bible doesn't give us all the answers we want. If we had all the answers, there wouldn't be any need for faith. We'd be God ourselves.

One thing more. After reading this book you'll wish, as I did, that you knew the Giesbrechts personally and had some kind of relationship with them. But even if you never meet them face to face, your wishes will come true to this extent: You'll really feel as I did, that you know the Giesbrechts. And you'll come to love them as I did.

1

"Chosen by Jehovah"

The little central Minnesota community where I grew up was much like the one described so graphically by Garrison Keillor. The fictitious location of Lake Woebegon is very near Rose City. Some of Keillor's fans were asking the locals recently to be directed to Lake Woebegon. If I'd been there I would've said, "You're here folks. Rose City is as close as it gets!"

On this beautiful crisp summer day my mother and my two older sisters and I were baking pies and caramel rolls and enjoying the relaxed routine of summer vacation after another year in school. "Sixth grade!" I whispered the magic words to myself as I washed the baking dishes in hot sudsy water. Although I had two younger brothers, being the third girl in my family, and a puny one with a crooked smile at that, had always made me wish I were older. It seemed all the power in the family had been out of my reach. As a sixth grader I'd at last be seen, like I looked up to my sisters.

Nancy and Debbie, the cousins who were closest to my age, and I, often lamented our lot of being younger sisters. It helped to have cousins to talk with when "the girls," as my older sisters were called, were invited to go with the pastor or church youth leader to some event, and I was not included. Sometimes I would answer the phone and be asked, "Do the girls want a ride to the Youth for Christ rally?" I always wondered, "Haven't they noticed I'm a girl, too?" But, Nancy and Debbie had the same problems. We understood each other.

All of my dad's seven brothers and sisters and their families lived within five miles of us, most of them were dairy farmers like us. Our close Swedish family system brought a special sense of "belonging" to a group who called you their own. Between celebrating each person's birthday and attending church together several times a week, my seventeen first cousins and I spent almost as much time together as if we had been raised in the same family.

Our world was small and relatively unaffected by the fast technological pace of metropolitan St. Paul/Minneapolis, 150 miles to the south. When we'd discuss the news it didn't necessarily mean the network news, but NEWS! Like, who showed up for church cleaning day, the neighbor's cows getting out and stomping my aunt's tomatoes, my grandma coming down with a chest cold. Important things. At least they were important to us in the tiny village of Rose City.

The people in my home church, a small evangelical fellowship, were the kind who would be available if anyone needed help. If a farmer had an appendicitis operation at harvest, neighbors would leave their own ripe fields while they gathered their equipment and brought in his crop. The women of the community would provide huge savory meals at noon and supper with hearty snacks between. Even so, our Scandinavian stoicism prevented us from being openly affectionate to one another or revealing our feelings.

On this particular summer day, however, my feelings were neither in check, nor hidden, as I whistled while washing the sticky caramel mixture from the silver pans, imagining all the while my elevated status as a sixth grader. The phone rang in the kitchen as I rinsed the last pan. "I'll get it," Mom called.

Turning from the sink I saw the horror in her face as I heard, "NO! Not Nancy!"

Everything stopped in that moment. My hopes and dreams of sixth grade grandeur. My innocent childhood belief that if you trusted God enough He would bless you and all would be well. I knew even before Mom said the words that my playmate and cousin, Nancy, had died. Nancy, though diabetic, had lived what seemed to me a normal life. She went to school, played with friends, attended church, and loved God. The medical terminology describing her death as complications from diabetes was not nearly as important to me as why would God "allow her to die?" How could it be? Nancy loved God as much as I did. I ran to my room slamming the door so I could be alone to cry. I felt overwhelmed with guilt for the times I'd been nasty to Nancy—times when I'd left her out of our cousin threesome. I felt a nagging painful guilt that I was alive and she was dead.

In the days before the funeral I continued to ask the question, "Why? Why did God let her die?"

My questions were answered, "We don't understand, but we trust that God knows what He is doing. He has called her home."

I wondered then, Why does God "call home" someone so young with so much life ahead of them? I remembered my little cousin Tommy. Such a beautiful blonde baby. Even though they lived fourteen miles from us, whenever I saw him I would fight for a turn to hold him or take him for a walk. When he died in a car accident, still an innocent toddler, I heard, "God calls some children home because they are the most special and He needs them in heaven."

With the loss of Nancy, I struggled again to understand why children die. Why does God need all of those children anyway? How could anything they do for God be worth the pain I saw in my aunt's and uncle's faces as they buried their children? (Norman, Nancy's older brother, had died eight years earlier, also of a diabetic complication.)

Why had my own family been spared? Had God especially favored us? Or were we just lucky? Indeed, my mother with empathy in her voice would also ask,"Why has God blessed us? We have been so fortunate. It just doesn't seem fair."

After Nancy died we rarely spoke of her. In our family system we never learned how to share any significant feelings. Even in grief we didn't feel free to let our emotions loose. Each of us had our private thoughts and memories about Nancy, but we implicitly obeyed the unspoken "NO TALK RULE." We acted as if she had never existed.

We mistakenly thought that if we "brought it up" we'd make Nancy's family feel bad. Although kind in intent, this only denied them permission to grieve in front of us, even though Nancy's family must have felt incredible pain long after the funeral was over.

Two years after Nancy's death, my questions about the suffering of children surfaced again.

Pammy, Nancy's sister, was a beautiful toddler with black curly hair and huge round brown eyes. Her happy disposition and dark coloring, unusual in our predominantly Scandinavian community, made her a favorite of everyone. The affection and feelings our Scandinavian heritage prevented us from expressing to older children and adults, we lavished on the babies in our family. Pammy was no exception.

I was visiting my grandma when the call came. As if it were today, I can hear Grandma cry, "Oh no! How can it be?"

It was difficult for all of us to believe. Pammy had come down with a cold only the night before. The next day her mother called the doctor to the house because Pammy had an elevated temperature and wasn't breathing normally. He admitted her to the hospital confirming their suspicions of pneumonia. She died the same day. The diagnosis was "quick pneumonia."

The girls' trio, made up of one of my sisters and two cousins, sang the old hymn, "When He Cometh" at Pammy's funeral. I listened to the words carefully trying to discern a clue to the "reason" for Pammy's death.

> *When he cometh, when he cometh To make up His jewels,*
> *All his jewels, precious jewels, His loved and His own.*
> *Like the stars of the morning, His bright crown adorning,*
> *They shall shine in their beauty, Bright gems for His crown.*

My heart cried out to God. *"It isn't fair! Jewels for your crown? There has to be a better reason than this for babies to die!"*

My world enlarged as I attended junior and senior high school at Parker's Prairie, a town about fourteen miles from my home. I made friends outside of the tiny community of Rose City for the first time noting many differences in the lifestyle and religious beliefs of my friends. I strove to become a model student, trying again to live up to the status of my sisters, both of whom were valedictorians of their class.

In my struggle to be more than "the little sister" I eventually developed leadership skills which I used in our church youth group, 4-H club, and in various school groups. Between those responsibilities and studies, piano and voice lessons, sewing projects, farm chores and babysitting jobs, it was easy to submerge my feelings in activity and work as did my relatives before me. For the time, my questions about suffering emerged only rarely. One such occasion was when I read the book, *The View From A Hearse*, by Joseph Bayly. I was so impressed with Mr. Bayly's candor in sharing the death of his three sons, in fact, I used it as a theme for a devotional message to my church youth group. His views about death and suffering seemed more logical than any I had heard before. Certainly more logical than other explanations of suffering I'd heard, such as, "It will make you a better person, or God has a purpose for each thing that happens—you'll understand someday."

While in my senior year in high school, I begged God to direct me to a college. Confused by the choices available, I finally wrote to Arthur Anderson, the dean at Oak Hills Bible College, with questions about credit transfer and applicability of their English Bible major to my chosen vocational interest in psychology. Oak Hills' only major was English Bible with a heavy emphasis on philosophy and logic.

Mr. Anderson responded by encouraging me to find a college more in line with my aspirations. Oak Hills, he said, was not accredited and though credits transferred well to some schools, it still might not be the best place for me.

The fact that Mr. Anderson put my interests before his own made me think Oak Hills might have some of the answers I'd been looking for.

Set in the Minnesota north woods and surrounded by lakes, Oak Hills seemed a natural place for spiritual, intellectual, and social development. I enrolled in the fall of 1973. The small school setting made it easy to get to know every student in a relatively short time. I noticed Tim during the opening week. Of medium build, his thick dark hair and olive complexion caught more eyes than mine. In fact, the first time I actually talked to him I was dating another boy and arranged for a friend of mine to double date with Tim. As the four of us shared a large pepperoni pizza at a local pizza shack, Tim and I were amazed at how much we had in common.

On a beautiful fall day, the following week, Tim asked to walk me back to my dorm. The walk turned into a three hour talk as we stopped to sit in front of one of the lakes, surrounded by beautifully colored oak and birch trees waving their leaves in welcome. The fact that Tim was Canadian, sensitive, intelligent, and incredibly good looking, only increased my interest in him.

As we shared together that day, Tim told me about his childhood. How his parents were Mennonite missionaries, until the mission board decided Menisino, a remote part of Canada, wasn't a profitable place for mission work. His parents disagreed and began to support their mission work by farming."

"My dad's a farmer," I said. "I bet we have a lot in common."

Tim smiled. "Probably not the quality of the land. Menisino soil is sandy and *full* of rocks. Some of our fields had twenty huge piles of rocks."

"Did you have to pick them?" I asked.

"I, and my three brothers, did more rock picking than I care to remember."

"Then we do have a *lot* in common," I laughed. "From the time I was thirteen I counted the number of fields I'd have to pick rocks from before I graduated from high school."

Tim went on to tell me how he and his six siblings walked a mile each way to school, saving on shoes by going to school barefoot in the early fall and spring. With seven children to feed, money could not be wasted.

He recalled how he had helped his brothers farm the rocky soil, while their father made visits to neighbors and invited them to worship in the tiny church on his farm. When a tractor didn't work, it was the boys who improvised until it ran again.

When Tim was a senior in high school the family finally left Menisino, moving nearer to the city of Winnipeg to run a large poultry farm. About the time of Tim's high school graduation it was decided that Tim would handle the farm's nine thousand chickens, while his father went to finish high school back in Menisino. I met Tim two years later when he was a second year student at Oak Hills.

Tim was my first and only love. Our courtship seemed almost storybook like. Indeed, Oak Hills surrounded on two sides by Upper and Lower Lake Marquette provided an idyllic setting for a romance. Although we both worked to put ourselves through college and traveled in separate musical groups we still managed to spend time playing, laughing and dreaming of our future together.

I was visiting Tim's family in Winnipeg when I had my first premonition that our backgrounds were in some ways very different. My family was always bustling around with some project. Supper time was a time to hurry and eat and get on with our work. In Tim's family supper sometimes lasted two hours as everyone talked together. Then two hours later Tim's mother served evening tea and they'd talk again.

Tim's father, a kindly man in his early sixties, loved to talk about God. One evening we were having tea after dinner and I mentioned that whenever there was a thunderstorm my parents asked us to sleep downstairs on the floor—just in case of fire. Tim's father was obviously shocked. "Don't they have faith in God?" he asked.

"Well, yeah," I mumbled, "but that doesn't mean nothing bad will ever happen to you, or that you shouldn't take precautions."

Tim's father quoted Bible verses about trusting God and being held in the palm of his hand. I thought of my cousins' deaths, but obeyed the "no talk rule," even though far removed from my family, and said nothing.

At Oak Hills we often discussed the problem of evil. "Mr. T.," as we called Mr. Thompson, the president of Oak Hills, was a deeply intelligent and logical man. Under his leadership the faculty pushed us to understand who God was for ourselves, instead of blindly accepting the traditions of our heritage. We came to believe that the free will of humankind was really free. For the first time I understood I could make true choices, that God could work through my choices, that in fact, He had chosen to do just that. I also began to understand that evil resulted from sinful humanity, that our capacity to choose between good things was also a capacity to make bad choices which often resulted in suffering for ourselves and others.

When I graduated from Oak Hills I had made huge strides in intellectualizing about the problem of evil. I continued to pray and think, however, as if God were the Big Santa Claus in the sky. Old habits and ways of thinking are very difficult to break.

A month after graduation from Oak Hills, Tim and I were married in a beautiful ceremony, repeating the vows we had written to each other. Although we promised to be faithful in sickness and distress, it never occurred to me that anything bad would ever happen to us. After all, we were Christians and surrendered to doing God's will. I pushed memories of my past heartaches from my mind.

As Pastor Jim Brown pronounced us man and wife and we marched out to ringing church bells and the anthem, "To God Be The Glory," I had never been happier.

Our first two years we lived in newlywedded bliss. Tim, the provincial manager of a security firm in Canada, enjoyed the responsibility of his job, and was rewarded with high praise from the national office. I worked as a preschool teacher and sometime assistant director at Mini Skools in Winnipeg. The ten three-year-olds in my classroom filled my life with hugs, smiles, and innocence.

Although we loved our jobs, both Tim and I had a desire to be involved in a Christian ministry. Tim's dream was to become a Christian radio broadcaster. To make this a reality Tim needed to finish his B.A. degree. He believed the best program for Christian broadcasting was at Northwestern College in St. Paul, Minnesota.

Our plan to move was exciting to me because I would be closer to my family. My only reluctance was leaving my children at Mini Skool.

It was while teaching at Mini Skool, that Pat, a fellow teacher mentioned her plans to start her own family center in Trinidad where she and her husband were returning soon. I hurried home from Mini Skool that day excited. "Tim! Tim! Pat gave me a great idea. I know how I can support you when you go back to college."

"Oh yeah?" Tim smiled at my enthusiastic chattering—such a contrast to his own quiet personality.

I had never heard of family daycare before, but soon discovered I could meet the qualifications easily. When we realized I could work at home we decided to begin our family.

Nine months later, we were settled in a small home on Cottage Place, just two miles from Northwestern College, anxiously awaiting the birth of our first child. Tim attended classes full time, while I supported us with "Penny's Daycare."

On Friday, February 10, 1978 I was discouraged to be ten days past my due date and weary of answering the phone to hear again, "Are you *still* home, Penny? *When* is that baby going to come?" I felt especially tired and crampy, but assumed it was only due to another eleven hour working day. Nevertheless, I laid on the couch in obvious discomfort.

As Tim monitored the minutes between my cramps he kept asking, "Do you think this is it, Honey?"

"After as many false alarms as we've had, I'm not making any predictions," I replied wearily. The cramps, however, soon became pains and only a short time later I carefully climbed in a wheelchair upon arriving at Midway Hospital in St. Paul.

Labor was more painful than anything I'd ever imagined. Tim cooled my forehead with damp washclothes, breathing with me rhythmically.

"Penny, I'll never forget what you're doing today. I love you!" he kept encouraging.

A few long hours later, an eight-pound-four-ounce baby boy lay on my tummy. Although we knew the rest of the human race had been born the same way, the birth of "our baby" seemed so spectacular—as if no one had ever been born this way before. *Is this what they call a natural high?* I wondered. Jeremy was so beautiful. So tiny. Surely, we had been partners with God in this grand culmination of our love.

"What's his name?" the doctor beamed, as proudly as if he were the new father.

Tim looked at us with tear glazed eyes as he answered, "Jeremy Charles. Jeremy means, 'Chosen by Jehovah.' "

Indeed, it seemed he was chosen by God just for us. I examined his tiny toes and fingers, his dark shock of hair, and big blue eyes. Joyous tears trickled down my cheeks, as I stared at our absolutely perfect son.

Three days later, Valentine's Day, seemed an appropriate time to bring Jeremy home, the fruit of our love. The snow sparkled in the bright sunlight as we drove along in our big green Ford sedan.

I smoothed Jeremy's long dark hair. "Tim," I whispered, "can you believe this is our own baby? Ours to keep."

Tim lovingly squeezed my arm. "Yeah, ours to keep. Our very own."

2

"Please Don't Take My Baby"

Our euphoria continued. Jeremy was a contented baby and needn't have been held constantly, but holding him was such a treat. I felt like a little girl eating hoarded candy.

The day after coming home from the hospital with Jeremy, I decided to go grocery shopping. Tim was not easily convinced that this was a good activity for a woman who had delivered a baby five days before. Finally he relented and in my typically independent Scandinavian spirit, I backed our Ford sedan out of the driveway, turning back only to look fondly at our little green bungalow. Although it boasted only two bedrooms, a kitchen, living room, bath and utility room, it was a cozy house. Cottage Place seemed an appropriate street name for our cottage-like home.

Finished with my shopping, I started for home somewhat more tired than I had anticipated I'd be. I began to cry. *Why am I doing this?* A lurking fear deep inside erupted as exhaustion overcame me. I remembered Pammy.

I began to sob, *"No, God! No! Please don't take my baby! Not like Pammy!"* My fear was not one without reality. I knew it could happen.

Jeremy is going to die! The thought kept pushing through my mind.

No! He is just fine. He's home with Tim right now, I argued with myself.

Just wait and see! my guilty self interrupted. *You love Jeremy more than you love God! He's going to get you for it!* My sobs echoed in the big car. Was it true? How could one feel the same emotion for an invisible God as for a little baby one could smell, touch, and feel?

I drove faster now, intent on my destination. Surging around the corner of Cottage Place, I whipped into our driveway and leaped from the car. Darting in the front door, with smeared makeup and swollen red eyes, I shouted, "Is he all right?"

Tim looked at me incredulously, "You were only gone half an hour! Of course he's okay! But what is *wrong* with you?"

Struggling to communicate the depth of my anxiety, I gasped, "Tim, I was so afraid. I thought he died. I just had this feeling he was going to die!" I sank weakly into a chair.

Tim sighed. "So this is what they mean by the postpartum blues."

Nature had it's way during the five weeks following my bout with postpartum depression. A normal hormonal balance returned to my body and my anxieties about Jeremy's well-being subsided.

While Tim studied, I cuddled and played with Jeremy.

"GOOOOHH! GOOOOOH!" he'd coo and gurgle.

I would respond, "GOOOOOH! GOOOOOOOOH! MAMA! Can you say Mama yet, Smart Baby?"

The pre-school children I cared for in my family daycare home were as enthralled as Tim and I, by the new addition to Penny's Daycare. However, Mark, in kindergarten, had reservations about "that dark purply thing on Jeremy's tummy." Day after day his finger paintings came from school with a stickman like blob in the center of the paper and a huge purple appendage circling it's entirety.

One day curiosity overwhelmed me and I asked, "Mark, Honey, Tell me the story of your picture."

He said proudly, "It's Jeremy and his cord!"

Indeed, our lives seemed full with Jeremy, my "borrowed children," and Tim's schooling going well. Nothing to warn us of the coming days.

Jeremy was one day short of being five weeks old when he developed symptoms of his first cold. He ate well when I nursed him, but seemed a little sniffly when I put him down for the night.

That evening I was awakened by Jeremy's cries, "Waaaaaaaaaah! Waaaaaaaaaaah." A gurgly sound of liquid running down his throat interrupted his wail. He seemed to be gasping for breath.

I shook Tim's shoulder. "Honey!" I shouted. "Wake up. Jeremy's sick!" Tim yawned as he reached over and gently touched Jeremy's forehead. "Let's take his temp'. He doesn't feel too warm."

Although Jeremy's temperature was only 101 degrees I was still concerned about his uneven breathing and the liquid I could hear him swallowing as it ran down his throat. The memory suddenly hit me again of Pammy dying of quick pneumonia, as I watched Jeremy gurgling and struggling to breathe.

The next hour passed and still Jeremy slept fitfully, waking each time he choked on the liquid running down his throat. I was worried. Carefully I picked him up from the homemade cradle that hung near our bed. I moved him to my shoulder, patting him lightly on the back, and using my other hand to flip through the pages of Dr. Spock's baby care book until I came to infants and fevers.

Anxiety rising, I woke Tim who had fallen back asleep. "Tim, Dr. Spock says babies five weeks old shouldn't run fevers, period, and if they do to call a doctor immediately!"

Tim groaned. "Penny, I don't think it's necessary. He doesn't have a high temp'. Besides, it's two-o'clock in the morning. Why bother to call the doctor? What can they do tonight?"

"Tim, if he *dies* because you won't call the doctor, I'll never forgive you." Tim's eyes widened in surprise at my anger. As soon as the words were spoken I longed to retrieve them.

"Okay." Tim got up quickly, "If it will make you feel better, I'll call."

Tim had grown up in a family with a different attitude toward getting medical help. With seven children and a missionary budget, a doctor visit, forty miles away, was reserved for only the most serious illness. Tim was also raised to believe that if you had enough faith in God, nothing bad would happen to you or your children. Their own family history supported that belief. There had never been a need to question it.

I *knew* people I loved could die. Tim had no experience with that. The naive belief we shared, however, was that it wouldn't happen to us.

Finally Tim called the hospital. The intern he spoke to was not familiar with the stage of baby development noted by Dr. Spock. He simply advised us to keep Jeremy cool, put him in an upright position, and bring him to the clinic the following day if he hadn't improved by morning.

Jeremy did seem better the next morning and some of our earlier fear subsided. In fact, we agreed Tim would go to school to take an early spring quarter exam, while I made arrangements for my daycare children and called the clinic for an appointment.

Upon hearing our report of the night before, Dr. Carolyn Levitt said quickly, "Get him down here immediately. Who was on call last night anyway?"

We hurried to the clinic adjoining St. Paul Children's Hospital and became increasingly concerned, when first one doctor examined him, then another. "Yes, he has an ear infection. Yes, he has pneumonia. I'm sorry Mr. and Mrs. Giesbrecht, but your baby needs to be hospitalized."

Jeremy seemed to droop even as we watched. Tim made the hospital arrangements as I waited alone, holding Jeremy close to my heart. He was sleeping now. His tiny face was white.

Silently I prayed, *How does it all fit? Are You trying to warn me not to love Jeremy too much? Jesus, what can I do? I want to trust Jeremy's life with You, yet I don't even understand what it is I should believe?* My head folded over Jeremy's sleeping white form, as I sat in the now empty and dimly lit waiting room. *Dear God in Heaven, What did I do to lose Your blessing? Everyday I pray for Your protection for my son. Why is this happening to us?* The tears from my eyes meandered to meet those from my nose.

My war with God continued until all of my arguments had been stated. Finally, spent, I sat resigned. *I've no one else to turn to. I don't understand anything about how You work. But, even if You do call children home . . . even if You call Jeremy home, You're all I've got. I choose to trust You.* A measure of peace overcame me. I was tired of fighting.

When Tim returned we walked slowly to the elevator leading to the hospital ward where we would leave our son. The doors closed behind us as if to shut out forever our mistaken belief that "nothing bad would ever happen to us."

Tim led me to Jeremy's room. A friendly nurse said, "Hi, you must be Jeremy's mom. Would you like to change him into a hospital gown or would you like me to?"

"I'll do it." I smiled through my tears as I silently pulled the tiny hospital kimono over Jeremy's head and took a diaper from Tim. A mother for only five weeks, I was back again in a crowded hospital room. Warm tears slid from my eyes, falling onto our baby's listless form.

Dr. Levitt walked in with a couple of younger doctors trailing behind. She bent over Jeremy. "Jeremy's a very sick child," she pronounced, "and at a critical age. We need your permission to do a spinal tap to check for spinal meningitis."

"Dr. Levitt," I asked anxiously, "Is he going to be okay?"

She threw her waist length blonde hair over her shoulder as she stood up and repeated kindly, "Jeremy's a very sick baby, Mrs. Giesbrecht. We'll just have to wait and see."

I nodded, wondering vaguely if anyone had noticed that my nose was running. I really didn't care and I hadn't the energy to ask for Kleenex. Nothing mattered now. Nothing but that Jeremy recover. Recoiling at the shock of my son's illness, I felt rudely shoved from the naivete of childhood to the reality of adulthood. *I'm only twenty-two-years-old! I'm too young to have to deal with this.* I struggled to remember what the doctor had said. "Spinal meningitis." What was that?

Tim and I signed the consent forms for the spinal tap and began one of the loneliest periods of our lives. How could it be only five weeks since we had experienced the ecstasy of the birth of our son?

The doctors took Jeremy out for the delicate procedure and then returned him to his room. "WAAAAAAAAHH! WAAAAAAAAAH!" he cried loudly.

True to nature, my milk came in upon hearing his cries. "Can I nurse him now?" I asked. "Maybe that will calm him."

"Sounds like a great idea," the nurse agreed, handing me the tiny bundle she carried. Jeremy's thick dark hair and deep blue eyes starkly contrasted with his pale white skin. Although he continued to cry, his fine features didn't take on the reddened appearance of a crying baby. But as I nursed Jeremy the reality of his illness became even more apparent. Normally a voracious eater, he sucked lethargically for a few moments, then dropped off to sleep. I looked up at the lithe form of my husband. "Tim, he just isn't eating. I can't get him to wake up!" My voice broke.

A young nurse popped in to say, "We're going to prepare your baby for an I.V. We will probably use a vein in his head so that we won't have to restrain his arms and legs as much."

"What will you run in the I.V.?" Tim asked.

"We'll be giving him large doses of antibiotics to fight off whatever is going on in there. You may want to leave while we do this. It isn't going to be pleasant."

"No, I'm staying. He'll know my voice," I said.

Tim nodded his agreement, "It might help."

"Suit yourselves. One of you may as well help hold him down then."

We watched tiny Jeremy fight and scream, writhing in agony as they tried to put the I.V. needle in his head. We tried to soothe him, but his eyes remained huge with terror. Holding down his little limbs that were fighting this newest invasion to his body, I tried to block from my heart his agonized cries, "Waaaaaaaaaaaahh! Waaaaaaaaaaaaah!"

Would it ever be over?

"Let's try another one. It's difficult to get the needle in an infant's tiny veins," the young doctor said grimly. Finally, after nearly an hour the ordeal was over. Dwarfed by the high stainless steel crib, Jeremy lay exhausted in a tiny heap.

Dr. Levitt encouraged me to continue the breast feeding. "Jeremy would probably be even worse if he hadn't had your immunities from the breast milk," she mused.

"I have some frozen milk at home. Could you use that when I'm not here?" I asked.

"Sure, that would be good. We want to do everything we can for him." Dr. Levitt paused, apparently sensing our anxiety. "The reason we're being so cautious with Jeremy is his age. We're especially wary when a four-to-six-week-old baby becomes sick. These two weeks seem to be the time an infant switches from the mother's immune system to his own. As a result, the infant's own antibodies aren't built up yet. Forty-eight hours will tell the story for Jeremy. We'll have the results of the spinal tap by then and we'll also know how he's responding to antibiotics."

Three wire plugs were glued to Jeremy's chest. These were connected to a monitor which would report to the nurses' station any irregularities in the vital signs. If the warning beep sounded, a nurse would know instantly that the patient might be in trouble.

We asked if we could stay with Jeremy that first night, but the hospital staff compelled us to go home.

"We'll take good care of him," the head nurse assured. "You two go and get some rest. Besides, there's not a thing you can do for him anyway."

It was nearly midnight when we left our little son with wires and tubes extending from his head and tummy. A small paper cup perched on the top of his head protected the I.V. needle from being accidentally pulled out. His arms and legs were restrained as added insurance that the needle wouldn't be jarred. With his limbs extended by restraints and the paper cup for a hat, he looked like a tiny mechanical doll.

We pulled into our driveway about midnight. While Tim put the car in the garage I went directly to Jeremy's room. Staring into his empty crib I sank to the floor and leaned my head against the shiny white crib rails. I thought of all the reasons for suffering I had read and heard in my childhood. "Pain makes us better people." "God chastises those whom He loves." "We don't understand God's ways." "God has a reason for everything that happens." "Nothing comes to us in life without passing first through the hand of the Father." "Someday we'll understand." The words seemed hollow and confused to me now.

The next morning Tim and I woke early and drove to Children's Hospital. We hurried to Jeremy's room. Nurses came in and out, weighing Jeremy's diapers to record output of fluid, checking his temperature, and monitoring his I.V. Carefully, Tim and I arranged Jeremy and his trailing tubes and wires, so I could continue to nurse him. Neither of us left him except to eat in the cafeteria.

Forty-eight-hours seemed an interminable amount of time to wait for news of the spinal tap. Given Jeremy's age and the fact that I was nursing him the doctors' concern was that Jeremy might have viral spinal meningitis rather than bacterial meningitis, which can be successfully treated with antibiotics. If the spinal tap showed viral meningitis the prognosis was grim.

"What will you do if he has the viral kind?" we asked.

"We'll wait and see what happens. Try not to worry about that now. The best thing you can do for Jeremy is to encourage him to nurse."

Most of our family members lived out of town, although my mom was on the way to help with Penny's Daycare on Monday. The phone rang frequently as they offered their support. As soon as Jeremy was hospitalized, Tim had called the pastor of the small church where we were youth group leaders, but neither the pastor nor anyone else from the church contacted us all weekend. We spent most of the hours waiting alone. As time passed, we wondered, "If they don't care enough to be with us when our son might be dying, when will we be important enough?"

Sunday morning when we walked into Jeremy's room he looked at us and actually smiled! It was his first real smile. We were encouraged and celebrated by having our own church service. Tim and I took turns holding Jeremy carefully in our arms, so we wouldn't dislodge the I.V. needle. We sang "Jesus Loves Me" and every other Gospel chorus we could remember. The singing and our touch seemed to comfort him.

While Jeremy slept we visited with other parents whose children were hospitalized, some for pneumonia, others for various minor surgeries, and still others because of terminal illness.

We also read magazines to pass the long, lonely hours, and

were astonished to note two stories in *Redbook* about young children being hospitalized. One mentioned that it is common for parents of hospitalized children not to visit them.

We had noticed the absence of many parents during our short time at Children's Hospital. The article explained the reason for this was because parents feel such enormous guilt for their children being sick and irrationally believe their children will be better off without them.

I realized I had felt much the same way in the initial hours of dealing with Jeremy's illness. I too, had felt incompetent of being a mother and wondered if Jeremy would be better off without me. I believed, that as Jeremy' mother, I was totally responsible for his welfare. When Jeremy got sick it seemed natural to blame myself.

The guilt I felt was so intense, I couldn't talk about it to anyone, not even Tim. After reading in *Redbook* that it was normal to feel guilt, I realized for the first time since we had arrived at Children's Hospital, that his illness might not be my fault. Jeremy's illness might have just happened.

Children's Hospital was being moved in a few months to a new building. The hospital seemed extremely short-staffed. We were told it was a way of saving money for the move. The lack of available nurses resulted in Jeremy's I.V. bag not being checked regularly enough. Several times the I.V. infiltrated causing blood to back up in the tube. This almost always meant the needle had to be reinserted. Although we were exhausted from coming to the hospital early in the morning and leaving at midnight after Jeremy's last feeding, we hardly dared leave him to go home to sleep. Each time we did, it seemed the staff would forget his I.V. The hour of agony it took to reinsert the I.V. needle was too great a price to pay for more rest.

By Sunday night the I.V. had already been restarted twice. Since my mom had come to take over Penny's Daycare, Tim and I decided that I should spend the night at the hospital and watch it myself.

Tim left and I collapsed on my cot exhausted. I was almost asleep when the alarm of Jeremy's vital signs' monitor jarred me back to reality. I jumped out of bed and shook Jeremy to make sure he was breathing. By the fifth time the monitor sounded with Jeremy still breathing normally, the nurses and I made a pact to have the monitor checked first thing in the morning.

Toward the middle of the night, I was startled by the loud clang of a bell. "That dumb monitor!" I thought, groping for the light by Jeremy's crib. As the insistent clanging of the bell continued I realized it wasn't the same noise as the monitor's alarm. Scurrying feet and the slamming of doors sounded around me. Pulling on my robe, I ran to the door and peeked out. No one was there. All the doors were closed now. It was quiet. Had there been a fire? Did they think I'd get my baby out? Had everyone evacuated already?

I eyed the I.V. connected to a tall pole. I'd have to pull the needle if I carried Jeremy to safety. There was no way I could hold the baby, the monitor, and the I.V. pole.

"God, what should I do?" I cried out loud. A moment later I heard normal activity resume in the ward. I poked my head out of the door questioningly. "Only a fire drill," the nurse explained complacently.

Monday morning they gave us the lab results. Jeremy did not have meningitis, only pneumonia and severe ear infections. The response to the antibiotics seemed good and we could take him home after he had been on an I.V. for ten days.

Thrilled, I first called Tim who had gone to his morning classes at Northwestern College, and then Mom, home with Penny's Daycare.

As I hung up, our pastor strolled in with a big smile. "Well, how's it going?"

I explained the events of the past three days and our relief at hearing the lab report. Soon, he turned to leave.

"Thanks for coming up," I said. "It's so good to see a familiar face," although I wanted to say, "You're our pastor. Where have you been?"

I'll never forget his reply. "Oh, no problem, we had to come to the clinic downstairs for our baby's immunization shots anyway. We didn't have to make an extra trip."

As the days progressed Jeremy's weight began to build, color returned to his face, and he again nursed voraciously. Finally we were able to take him home from the hospital. Six weeks had passed since our first giddy ride home as a brand-new mom and dad. This ride was different. We were reverent in our joy. Jeremy's mommy and daddy had grown up. Images of the terminal children we had left behind at Children's Hospital only briefly flitted through my mind as I assured myself, *Nothing is going to happen to our baby after all. God is good. He's watching over Jeremy. Nothing bad is going to happen! Nothing!*

3

"Something's Wrong With Jeremy"

The warm April sun burst through my mother's sparkling clean windows. Baby Jeremy nuzzled his head close to my breast smiling contentedly now that his tummy was full. How good it felt to be snuggling my baby and enjoying the delight of my parents' love for their first grandson. The memory of Jeremy's recent illness was still poignant. I was grateful to God for I believed He had spared Jeremy's life. Occasionally, however, thoughts still haunted me of the terminally ill babies we had left behind at Children's Hospital—children, it seemed, who had not warranted the same blessing.

"Oooooh!" Jeremy cooed. I shook off the black feelings that had crept over me again.

"What is Grandpa up to now?" my mother exclaimed, looking out the window.

We heard a whinny from outside, then the door opened as Dad led our aging family pony, Buddy, through the breezeway and across the threshold of Mom's lovely kitchen. "I thought Jeremy might want a ride," he said with a sheepish grin.

"DeWayne!" Mom looked at Dad with disbelieving eyes. "Not in the kitchen!" But Dad already had Buddy inside. I laughed at my father's bold silliness so uncharacteristic of his stoic Swedish character.

"I thought Jeremy would like a pony ride," Dad explained and then added apologetically, "It's just too cold for him to be outside after he's just been sick and all."

"Well at least let me get the camera," Mom declared. "This will be a shot to remember!"

So at just seven weeks, Jeremy had his first pony ride in my parents' big farm kitchen. Dad had insisted on keeping Buddy—"for the grandkids," he said—long after we children had outgrown him.

Being Jeremy's grandfather brought Dad out of himself in a way I'd never seen before. "You want Grandpa don't you, Jeremy," he'd say taking him from my arms with confidence.

Mom also bragged unabashedly about Jeremy to anyone who would listen. She insisted Jeremy knew who his Grandma was as she'd calm him when he'd cry. "He's so beautiful, he could be a girl," she crooned patting his tiny back, "and so smart besides." Once I gave her a large framed picture of Jeremy which she carried in her purse. "After all, people want to see the latest picture of Jeremy. He changes so fast."

Jeremy was loved not only by my parents and Tim's, but by everyone who knew him. He was a naturally outgoing baby so wherever we went people ogled and cooed for the privilege of his special smile. Occasionally an older relative would remark, "He's so good it almost scares you, doesn't it?" Each time this was said a shudder would sweep through my body as I remembered hearing as a child, "God calls the very special children to heaven. They are like angels sent to earth as a gift for a short while."

Such worrisome thoughts and rememberances were easily swept aside as I stayed busy caring for Jeremy and the children in Penny's Daycare. All the children were older than Jeremy. I had decided early on I could best use my teaching skills by caring for only preschool children. Also, I wanted Jeremy to get all of the touch and attention an infant needs to thrive. I didn't believe I could do that with other infants and toddlers in my program.

When Jeremy was an infant I had three full time as well as several part time children enrolled in my program. The three little boys I cared for full time were all "only" children and were delighted to finally have a "brother."

Four-year-old Shane asked me one day, "Penny, why did ja name him 'Germy'? I thought you said Germy's give you a tummy ache."

David, only three, was also confused by the name and always referred to Jeremy as, "Germany."

Mark, at five, decided that he was entirely too old to be Jeremy's brother. He answered only to, "Uncle Mark."

All of Jeremy's admirers were particularly delighted when he began to talk.

"Dada" was his first word at five months, then, at eight

months, "Mama" and "Nana" (num-num) were added. By twenty-one months Jeremy was mimicking everything we said, although his favorite words were, tractor, Buddy-horsey, truck, and Grandpa.

We often said, "Oh, Jeremy, you are so precious." One day he responded with, "Papa, precious."

By Jeremy's second birthday, February 11, 1980, I was pregnant again. Initially I was thrilled. Another baby. Yet, with that joy a new thought shoved unbidden into my mind, *Jeremy won't get all my love and attention now. What had we done?* We had never entertained the idea of raising an only child, however, after Jeremy's birth our love for him seemed so exclusive and our family so complete that I was afraid. Could I ever love another child as I loved Jeremy?

I scurried around the kitchen getting dinner ready for his birthday party, glad that at last I was feeling energetic again. I didn't want anything, including the new baby growing inside of me, to adversely affect this special day for Jeremy.

Pushing these thoughts aside, I finished setting the table and tossed a fresh vegetable salad, all the while keeping a watchful eye on my daycare children busily playing with Jeremy and his new presents.

Our guests arrived with their daughter, Mandi, just three months older than Jeremy. She was an extremely mature child and was already bored with the age appropriate puzzle her family had given Jeremy for his birthday. Jeremy seemed more interested in playing with trucks and building trains with his blocks than doing puzzles.

I was weary by the time the party was over and Jeremy was tucked in for the night. Tim looked at the large stack of toys Jeremy had received and remarked, "Sometimes I kind of worry he's going to grow up and never know what it means to do without."

Tim knew.

As Tim and I lay in bed that night talking about our son's future and what direction our parenting should take, I thought again of Tim's childhood. We both knew the hurt the poverty had caused yet I wondered, had the improvising, fixing, and working together also honed him into the practical, patient, and dependable man I had married?

The concerns we had about materialism's effect on Jeremy became irrelevant as the year of 1980 progressed. Jeremy, normally so affectionate and happy, began to lie on the floor kicking and screaming for no apparent reason. Also, Jeremy hadn't learned any new words for some time. Still we believed it must be just a stage—surely these behaviors wouldn't persist. We refused to believe that our firstborn son was going to be less than a perfect child. Well, almost perfect. Though watchful, our concern was mild as we prepared for the birth of another baby. We decided Jeremy, a sensitive child, was only reacting to the expectancy in the atmosphere around him.

Tim graduated from Northwestern College in the spring of 1980 "flanked" by his nine-months' pregnant wife and two-and-one-half-year-old son.

A week later we welcomed Charity Joy to our family. Her dark beauty overwhelmed us. Often people remarked, "Her name should be Cherokee. She looks Indian."

Charity's bright red cherry lips showed up clearly on her birth pictures. When Shari, one of my daycare children, saw the pictures taken just hours after Charity's birth, she prayed, "Dear God. Please fix Baby Charity's sore lips."

Jeremy seemed tolerant of his new sister, but refused to call her Charity. His baby cousin's name was Benji. Jeremy stubbornly called her "Benji-girl" for months.

Charity's birth showed me that, indeed, I could love another child as much as I loved Jeremy. It didn't, however, lessen Jeremy's seeming fretfulness and lack of progressive development.

One day I spoke to my good friend, Sandy, on the phone, and for the first time shared our concerns about Jeremy. "Sandy, "You've got four kids. Did any of them ever quit saying new words at two-and-a-half?"

"No behavior should be judged as anything more than a stage until it lasts at least six months. Don't panic yet," she assured me.

Other friends also advised us not to worry, "It's only sibling rivalry," they said.

About two weeks after Charity was born, Jeremy stood in his room and pronounced, "I want to go to the farm today."

"Tim! Tim!" I shouted. "Jeremy just said a whole sentence. He said, 'I want to go to the farm today.' "

"You're kidding. Maybe we *should* go up to Rose City. We don't have anything special planned."

"Oh let's, Tim. He loves it up there so much this might help him want to talk. Maybe he'll realize how powerful language can be."

The car packed, I surveyed the living room for anything we might have forgotten. As I stooped to pick up Baby Charity sitting contentedly in her infant seat, Jeremy smiled smugly and waved, "Bye Bye Benji-girl!" His two-year-old mind could not comprehend that "Benji-girl" would share the attention of his grandparents as well as his Mom and Dad.

Jeremy had a good weekend at the farm and although he didn't speak again in long sentences we came home feeling good. Maybe we'd been overreacting to his lack of verbal progression.

Our sense of well-being was short lived. One Sunday a few weeks later when we picked Jeremy up from Sunday school his teacher said, "Jeremy doesn't seem to mingle with the other children. He normally plays by himself. Have you noticed this at home?"

Tim and I were perturbed. He's only two, we thought. Isn't there any room for individuality in our culture? Yet we began to watch him more closely and soon a lurking uneasiness hovered over us. Jeremy seemed reclusive, he played alone almost always, and he didn't giggle unless directly stimulated by someone.

A couple of old friends and their two children who came to visit for several days had their own explanation for Jeremy's regression. "I think," Dave pronounced one evening after Tim had finally gotten Jeremy to sleep, "Jeremy is not getting enough attention. I've been watching him all week and he just wanders around in his own little world."

I could see Tim's face tense as Dave spoke. Normally an easy going soft spoken man, Tim's anger rarely surfaced. His words now were intense and frank. "Your observations, Dave, have been made while Penny has had four extra people in her house for a week. When you called and asked if your whole family could stay with us and asked Penny to babysit your children everyday, that is precisely why we discouraged you. Both Penny and I try to spend every minute we can with Jeremy, but it's not easy with four extra people in the house." Tim paused for a moment as if surprised by his own unbridled emotion. "Don't you realize," he spoke gently now, "Penny and I are more concerned about Jeremy than anyone."

Although our hurt was tempered by the realization that their observation was made when they and their two babies lived with our family for ten days, we could not discount it altogether. We studied the possibility as objectively as possible and then decided to speak to a professional psychologist about the matter.

Marie Peterson, an elementary teacher in our school district and my dear friend, said, "Penny, if you're that worried why don't you have Henry Panowitsch see him? Henry's on the Mounds

View School District Early Intervention Team. He has a wonderful reputation and if Jeremy does need special help, Henry will be able to get it for him."

I called Dr. Panowitsch the next day and asked, "Is it possible my family daycare business could be the cause of Jeremy's regression?"

"I have seen that occasionally a child is not able to handle a parent caring for other children," he said in a distinct German accent. "An evaluation will be necessary to determine if this is the cause of Jeremy's behavior, however."

My conversation with Dr. Panowitsch reinforced in both Tim's and my mind that our recent decision to build a latchkey daycare center was the right one. Kids' Kottage Daycare Center, as we named it, would allow us to have a four hour working day during the months of the school year.

Tim's original career focus had now changed. Originally he had planned to be a Christian broadcaster, however the fact that he was a Canadian citizen would postpone the licensure he needed to be a broadcaster by at least three years. Although Tim had done very well in his classes, he also didn't feel sure anymore that being a Christian broadcaster was the best way to use his skills.

Tim had been raised to believe full time Christian work was the highest kind of vocation. He had received a B.A. in Christian Ministries and an Associate Degree in Broadcasting, and in the months following graduation he followed several openings for Christian ministry. He seriously considered one of those, a youth pastorate position, even though it would have meant moving from our home. After searching his heart, however, he realized his desire to be in a "full time ministry" were more reflections of his upbringing than dreams of his own.

Tim had grown to love the children as he helped in Penny's Daycare while attending college, and the children adored him. Slowly the seed idea grew in both of us of expanding Penny's Daycare to a fully state licensed center for latchkey children.

The idea kept developing as we explored building alternatives, set goals, sought licensing information, and realized the tremendous need in our community for a latchkey service. Kids' Kottage, if we succeeded, would be the only private solely latchkey daycare center in Minnesota. But our greatest desire was that we would have more time for Jeremy. Surely, he would now get all of the special attention and extra help he needed.

A friend had told me, "You can't give up, Penny. Einstein didn't talk until he was five and he became a genius." Surely,

Jeremy who could talk, had only a minor learning disability. Now that both Tim and I would be available to tutor him we would overcome his problems.

Tim was also supplementing our income by working as a security systems installer. This and plans for building Kids' Kottage Daycare Center had kept us so busy that our worries about Jeremy lessened for the moment. Starting a state licensed daycare center was a complicated venture. Eventually the foot-high paperwork with five government agencies was waded through, the red tape mostly cut, and Tim and I were certified as preschool and school age daycare center teachers. For financial and aesthetic reasons we had chosen to build Kids' Kottage Daycare Center onto our home. Our final obstacle would be to obtain a special use permit for a daycare center in a non-commercially zoned area. We broke ground for the center, saw our special use permit go through, and I took Jeremy to Dr. Panowitsch for a formal examination, all in the same week.

The day I drove up to the impressive circular school building for Jeremy's evaluation, I was optimistic that at last we would have the answers we needed to help Jeremy. I felt proud as Jeremy and I walked hand in hand up the sidewalk. Watching him skip beside me in his navy blue sailor suit, no one would have guessed that such a beautiful blonde three year old could have a problem in the world.

Marie had told me, "Henry Panowitsch is a great, big man, but he has the heart of a teddy bear." Her description of the fair, balding man with the German accent seemed appropriate. I liked him from the beginning.

Henry and two other early childhood specialists observed Jeremy's play while I completed the Alpern-Bell Developmental Profile test. The test placed Jeremy at about two years and five months of age developmentally, just eight months short of his chronological age. I was encouraged that Jeremy was so close to being age appropriate. However, our concerns of Jeremy's reclusiveness, inability to follow instructions, and crying tantrums, were also of concern to Henry, as he asked me to call him.

While one of the specialists cared for Jeremy, Henry and I sat down to talk about the evaluation.

Dwarfing the child-size chair he sat on, Henry began. "Jeremy is an unusual young man. When you and I speak, there is some kind of connection." He gestured sweeping his hand between us. "We understand in some way what the other means." He paused as he struggled to explain. "When I speak to Jeremy, it's as if he's not aware of what I say. The connection just isn't there."

Nervously I pushed my hair over my shoulder. "What do you think is the cause of this? Could the daycare be the problem?"

"Oh, no!" Henry exclaimed emphatically, "Oh my, no. There is nothing you could have done to make him like this. Something neurological is going on." Henry leaned back in his chair looking thoughtfully at me. "Let's do this thing. There is a pediatric neurologist at Children's Hospital who I think is very good with these kinds of difficulties. I will send him a report of our team's findings and request that a full workup be done, with medical, psychological, speech, language, developmental, and audiological components. After that we'll know more what is happening."

I looked at him, incredulous. *Neurological! What was he saying? Jeremy's only three!* Never had I considered Jeremy's problems to be anything more than a slight learning disability. *Something must really be WRONG with Jeremy. But, he is such a bright baby and toddler. Why everyone says so. Oh dear God. What will Tim think?*

As I drove home the tears pressuring my eyes and cheekbones stubbornly refused to flow. If only Tim had been with me, I thought. Neither of us had expected this to be a big deal.

Rounding the corner I saw Tim's car. Another man was with him. Tim had never come home in the middle of the day from his job as a security system installer. I rushed out of the car pulling Jeremy with me.

"Tim!"

"Hi, Hon," he called cheerfully. "I just brought Al over to see what we're building here since we were in the neighborhood."

Tears slipped from my cheeks as I grabbed my husband's hands. "Oh, Tim. They said something's wrong with Jeremy. Something neurological."

My words seemed wooden . . . mechanical. How could it be? Surely Henry was wrong. God would take care of the problem, whatever it was. He wouldn't allow Jeremy to be . . . My mind refused to even form the words.

4

No Answers

Two weeks after the evaluation Jeremy began screaming in pain one night during a party we were giving. One of the guests happened to be an R.N. and discovered that he had a huge hernia bulge. A hernia! Maybe this was all that was wrong with Jeremy. After all, it could explain the tantrums we'd noticed. Maybe the pain Jeremy was experiencing had caused his mysterious regression.

Elated, we immediately made an appointment with his doctor. A few days later surgery was scheduled. The simple day surgery seemed a small tradeoff for having our Punky Boy—as I often called him—back to normal again. The days following the hernia repair, however, our hopes were again dashed, for Jeremy showed no improvement in his level of frustration or communication skills.

It was becoming more and more obvious that Jeremy suffered severe developmental delays in his verbal communication even though occasionally his understanding would surprise us.

Sue Ann, one of our good friends, had given Jeremy a truck after his hernia surgery. A few weeks later she was at our house and asked Jeremy, "Where is your truck?"

Ten minutes later he silently handed it to her.

One of the most difficult problems we struggled to cope with was Jeremy's increasing hyperactivity. He pulled the curtains off his windows and dumped out all five of his baskets of toys. He loved to mix together the contents of several games. He dumped juice from a pitcher in the fridge and watched mesmerized as the sticky liquid poured out onto the floor. Constantly on the go, he repeated many such events several times a day. While we were cleaning up one mess, he would be off making another, or worse yet running out the door. Sometimes he'd walk right into a neighbor's house without ringing the bell.

The fact that we were building a daycare center only complicated our frustration with Jeremy's hyperactivity. Although Tim's brother Dan and family came to live with us for awhile and helped with the initial construction, financial constraints forced us to finish most of the remainder of the building project on our own.

We enjoyed the three weeks Karen and Dan spent with us far more than their enormous help on the building project. They were fun to be around and we needed to laugh. One night we'd all worked from morning till late at night. Even the children had helped sweep floors and carry lumber. Tim and Dan hooked up a long construction ramp from the second story of the addition. Soon we heard howls of delight as Tim and Jeremy sailed down the boards crouched in a small red wagon. Dan, pushing his Stephanie and Corey in a wheelbarrow, whizzed past us next. The lighthearted fun gave us the relief we needed.

Normally I spent days and evenings with Jeremy and Charity as well as operating Penny's Daycare. Since Jeremy's sleeping habits were erratic I would lay with him each night until he fell asleep, often not till eleven p.m. Then I'd get up and help Tim with drywalling, painting, or insulating.

We had to keep check on Jeremy every couple of minutes. One day when I searched the house and couldn't find him, I called to Tim for help. We combed the yards on our small, dead-end street, all the while calling, "Jeremy! Jeremy!"

"Mommy! Mommy!" he called. I could hear giggling, but couldn't see him even though I checked the garage, under the pool deck, and looked through the whole house. Eventually. . . I looked up. There was Jeremy running back and forth across the steep 6/12 pitch roof of our house above a cement walkout sixteen feet below him. A roof so steep even Tim is very cautious walking on it.

Tim raced to the ladder and made his way to Jeremy as fast as he safely could. Behind him at last, he squatted down and pulled Jeremy to his legs. I watched as they scooted slowly up and down the rooflines finally reaching the four-foot edge where Jeremy had begun his climb. Only later did we discover that Jeremy had climbed to the roof by leaning a heavy five-foot wooden ladder against the low edge of the four foot roofline, and from there scaling two roof peaks to arrive where I finally spotted him.

A few days later the clinic called verifying dates for a series of tests for Jeremy. Two months had passed since Henry's evaluation. We thought—we fervently hoped that maybe we'd at last find out what was wrong with our son.

Thankful for the small size of the new red Opel we now owned, I squeezed between two other cars in the crowded Children's Hospital parking lot. "Oh shoot, we're going to be late, Jeremy." Although I'd managed to find help to run Penny's Daycare so I could take Jeremy for his tests, it wasn't easy. My parents had offered to help when they could, but they had a farm to run and my sisters were busy with their own children.

Grabbing Jeremy out of the car, I ran down the hill to the entrance of the clinic Henry had recommended. We'd just have to do the best we could. We had asked the clinic to schedule Jeremy's tests within a couple of days so my mom could help with the daycare, but we were soon made aware that medical facilities don't run on patient time. A fact I was reminded of again as I tried to entertain Jeremy in the waiting room of the clinic.

"Jeremy Giesbrecht?"

The nurse's voice brought me back to the present. Testing was about to begin.

Dr. Deerborn, a young doctor, not much older than myself, gave Jeremy a thorough examination. He asked me, "Mrs. Giesbrecht, can you tell me the first time you had any suspicion something was wrong with Jeremy?"

"A Sunday school teacher talked to us about Jeremy's reclusiveness about a year ago. I think we had some premonition at that time something was wrong."

"What kind of concerns did you have?"

"Well, it was around then when Jeremy seemed to be fussy a lot. He had always been incredibly happy as a baby and toddler. We were confused."

"What do you mean by fussy? Temper tantrums?"

"No, he didn't ever seem angry, just upset. In fact, it seemed more like he was hurting somewhere. Maybe he was. We discovered a hernia just last month. But even since the surgery he continues to be fussy."

"Has Jeremy's hearing been tested?"

I smiled. "The million dollar question. Yes, it has. He does act a lot like he's deaf, but his hearing tests have repeatedly come back normal."

As I explained Jeremy's reclusiveness and hyperactivity Jeremy paced the small room, touching all the textures and picking up everything that moved. "Kind of like this," I laughed. "Always on the go."

"Is Jeremy aware of danger, Mrs. Giesbrecht? Does he, for instance, understand that he shouldn't run in the street?"

"No, not really. Jeremy wouldn't walk in front of a car if he was paying attention, but he doesn't always pay attention. We never know what he'll do for sure. This is just an example. Jeremy loves trucks. One day he saw a huge truck across a busy street and ran right over and began stroking it as if it were a favorite pet. We're so afraid he'll get hurt."

Dr. Deerborn chuckled as he noticed Jeremy peering up into his eyes. "He is a beautiful little boy, isn't he? That will help him along the way," he remarked kindly.

Nodding in agreement, I watched Jeremy tug at the shiny stethoscope and then race to pat the office door. "The thing that makes it so hard is that Jeremy's understanding is so limited, yet his coordination is remarkable."

"You don't feel he has lost skill in coordination?" Dr. Deerborn asked. He looked up briefly from writing in the chart.

"No, not at all," I laughed and told him briefly of the roof escapade.

After hearing this last story, Dr. Deerborn not only set up some of the other team tests the clinic and hospital would carry out, but also recommended family counseling to deal with the pressure of coping with our hyperactive son. Refusing to give up, we anxiously waited for results of the St. Paul Children's Hospital workup. Dozens of blood tests for remote regressive diseases came back negative. Psychological tests were futile because Jeremy didn't understand the verbal directions given to him. His level of speech was evaluated by a speech clinician who postulated that Jeremy's behavior might be an exaggerated case of sibling rivalry. But still nothing conclusive was discovered to explain Jeremy's mysterious regression.

We still believed someone would figure out what was wrong with Jeremy. We were willing to give up all we had to make it possible for him to get better. We read "miracle" stories in magazines, and books. Often people told us of this or that child who had been severely delayed and *now* was a genius. We decided *we'd* settle for good old average.

Continuing to hope for that clue that would unlock the mystery of our son's regression we took delight in Jeremy's uniqueness in a way only parents can.

During the middle of the testing at Children's we celebrated Charity's first birthday. Most of the guests had already left, when Jeremy came crying, "OWWWIIE!" He held his arm at a right angle to his body.

"What do you think, Jackie?" Tim asked my nurse sister. "Could it be broken?"

Jackie was always reluctant to give medical advice. "I don't know. Come here, Honey, and let me look at it."

"Owwiee!" Jeremy pulled his arm away.

"I'd take him in and get it X-rayed if I were you. He seems to be having a lot of pain."

Once again we made the familiar trip to Children's Hospital. This time at least we left with a medical answer. Jeremy had a broken arm and a cracked collar bone.

Wearily we crawled into bed that night. "Tim, between the seven kids in your family and the five kids in mine we had one broken bone and no really serious accidents or illnesses. I always thought it was because God had blessed our family. Now I wonder."

"Me, too," Tim responded softly. "Me, too." The broken thought hung between us as we each struggled to understand how God is involved in suffering.

Several days later when the radiologist had time to look at the X-rays, he disagreed with the diagnosis the emergency room doctor had given. Broken or not, by then the pain had subsided and the sling and collar had done their work. The diagnosis wasn't important anymore.

Watching Jeremy deal with the pain of blood tests, electric shock studies on his nervous system, and a myriad of other emotional and physical invasions, was becoming more than I could bear. I was so tired . . . so tired. His arm being hurt seemed the last straw. How could God have a purpose for all this?

My cousin, Lois, had many similar questions. The sister of Norman and Nancy and the aunt of Pammy, Lois was well acquainted with grief. Now, she was widowed at the age of thirty-six, having lost her beloved husband Bill who died while awaiting a kidney transplant.

Lois spent quite a bit of time with our family after Bill's death. She empathized with us in our heartache over Jeremy's regression and we in turn ached for her loneliness.

Part of the same family system in which I'd grown up, Lois felt the need to talk to someone about her pain in losing Bill and we felt that same need to share our fear, our pain, our loss. We struggled together to understand where God fitted into our suffering. Why were some people's lives so easy? Why were ours so difficult?

Lois had a friend with a big heart. She believed a puppy was the solution to Jeremy's problems and generously offered to give him a purebred American Eskimo pup. Although we had heard that dogs can be great for non-verbal kids, we had serious reservations about owning a dog in the city.

After careful consideration, we relented and Amy came to live with us. She nipped and barked, chewed on furniture, wet the rug and jumped up on everyone. Just as I had imagined! A dog does not belong in the city. But Jeremy loved her. He laughed and giggled as Amy chased him and sat on his lap forcing him to notice her.

Three days after Amy arrived, the owner's husband called to tell us he'd changed his mind. He wanted Amy back.

"It isn't fair!" I raged as I pitched Amy's favorite bone and dog blanket into a bag. I wanted so much to stand up to him. To say, "Look, you don't understand. Jeremy loves Amy!"

But when he came I said only, "Here she is. Jeremy's going to miss her."

We bought another tiny American Eskimo pup we named "Bambi," short for Baby Amy. Jeremy never took to Bambi as he did to Amy. We always wondered what he thought about when his dog left and if it would have made a difference if Amy had stayed.

Although Jeremy's facial expression often appeared blank, his sensitivity to what went on around him continued to amaze us. Each time Jeremy saw the needle come out to draw blood for still another series of tests he would scream, and struggle to escape the adults holding him down. Finally, resigning himself as the needle was inserted, he'd pathetically sing-song, "Jesus love Jeremy! Jesus love Jeremy!" My heart would break as I listened and watched.

It seemed to us, when he didn't understand what we were asking him, that he would grimace in a peculiar way, as if to say, "I'm trying; I just don't know what you mean."

One way Jeremy exhibited his insecurity was by crawling into bed with us in the middle of the night—that is, if he wasn't there already. Many times he fell asleep after we did and so for safety sake we put him in bed between us. It was the only way we could be sure he wasn't roaming the house, or worse, the neighborhood.

Jeremy's neurological evaluation was drawing to a close. The speech clinician's early diagnosis of an exaggerated case of sibling rivalry gave us great hope, but as the psychologist's report and lab tests came back it seemed more and more likely something was really wrong.

One of the last tests we had done required a twenty-four-hour urine specimen. It sounded easy at the clinic.

They showed me the little bags with a tiny hole for Jeremy's penis. Adhesive surrounded the hole to keep it in place.

"Remember," Joann, the nurse had said, "If you lose any we have to start over again in the morning."

"How much is any?" By now I was getting used to being prepared for what could go wrong."

"An ounce is too much to lose, Penny. Here, take this tape home and get the bag on really tight. Sometimes when kids urinate the adhesive gets wet and falls off."

We began the test the day of a family picnic. Carefully I watched for a sign Jeremy might be urinating. Unfortunately, bowel movements complicated the procedure, but we were doing well. Taking my urine bottle, (hidden in a brown paper bag) from our hostess's refrigerator I cautiously poured the contents of Jeremy's little bag into it.

The words, "Just be glad you don't have a girl," rang in my ears as I scrupulously taped on Jeremy's new bag.

Home again, I was relieved to know we had just three hours left to go. I turned to Jeremy to check the contents of his little bag, but I needn't have bothered. The front of his pants had a dark ring. Jeremy, though not potty trained, didn't urinate frequently. But when he did. . . . his little bag was just a bit too little. We lost more than an ounce.

We tried again the next day and then the next. Finally, the fourth day we managed twenty-three successful hours. I headed for Children's Hospital. This time I would not fail. We spent the last half hour in the lobby of Children's Hospital cautiously monitoring the bag. As I waited in the crowded lobby I realized Jeremy was urinating. I debated, "Should I take out the bottle right here in front of everyone, or should I be discreet and get Jeremy to the ladies room. I chose the latter. I lost more than an ounce.

Eventually the feat was accomplished. When this test result came back normal I had mixed feelings. Would we ever find out what was wrong with Jeremy?

On our last visit to Dr. Deerborn, we were to hear a combined report of the findings of the speech clinicians, audiologists, psychologists, blood tests, brain scan, EEG, and urine study. Tim and I walked in together. Maybe at last we'd know how to help our son be himself again. Tim held Jeremy's hand tightly. I carried one-year-old Charity with her head on my shoulder. She was by this time far out-talking her brother. I watched them silently. Jeremy jumped around in his navy sailor jump suit while Tim tightly held his hand in check. Charity's dark hair framed her round face. Heavy dark eyebrows set her apart from other toddlers. Her white pinafore covering her red dress made her olive skin glow. Both of my children are beautiful, I reflected. No one would ever guess, seeing us walk through the heavy revolving doors of Children's Hospital, the reason for our heavy hearts.

We introduced Dr. Deerborn to Charity, whom he had not seen before. He said, "It's easy to see that she's fine."

We wondered again if he had really believed us when we'd explained, "Jeremy used to be normal."

First, Dr. Deerborn reviewed the tests that had been done. I listened halfheartedly, already being more than familiar with the tests gone through. As I watched Jeremy pacing the room I heard the doctor saying, "The results to the nerve study were normal. The EEG did show some abnormality due to the slowing of the dominant posterior background for age and frequent left occipital spikes."

"What do you mean by abnormal, Doctor?" Tim asked.

"Well, it's inconclusive, a normal person could have the same brain scan; however this type of pattern occurs more frequently in people who are having some kind of seizure activity."

Abnormal! I listened intently as he continued. "We have tested Jeremy for every treatable regressive disease and all of the more common untreatable regressive diseases. All of these tests have come back negative. After speaking to the psychologist and speech clinician my feeling is this: There are three broad categories that children fall into who show a developmental delay. The first is non-specific retardation, far and away the largest; the second, psychiatric difficulties; and the third, degenerative disease. Often a history of regression turns out simply to be a lack of expected progression. In this case, however, you have given a fairly consistent history of loss of skills. Since the test results have come back negative, I think all we can do is wait and see."

Dr. Deerborn again suggested family counseling to deal with Jeremy's handicap, encouraging us as well to enroll him in our local Day Activity Center in the fall.

We left with wooden legs. We walked to the parking lot in silence. We had always thought we would find a cure.

Surely with our determination we would still find it. The doctors didn't know what was wrong. Maybe we would find the miracle cure on our own. God had always blessed our families. Surely He was just waiting to glorify Himself by healing Jeremy in a spectacular way.

Friends and family showered us with ideas they had read or heard about, sometimes sharing only a simple hunch. Many we pursued, others we disregarded.

One day I read a newspaper article about lead poisoning. The symptoms sounded similar to Jeremy's and it was *treatable.*

When I called Dr. Deerborn to inquire about it, he said, "It's unusual to find lead poisoning when the patient's family is from a middle-class suburban neighborhood. But, hey, it's an idea worth trying."

My feelings were scrambled as we waited for the test results. Lead poisoning treatment is a long and extremely painful process. I braced myself for that eventuality however, because I was almost sure this was finally what was wrong with Jeremy. Occasionally, thoughts crossed my mind about what kind of life Jeremy would have to look forward to if we never found out what was wrong. I shuddered to even think of it.

When the day came for the results to be in I dialed the clinic number shaking with excitement. "Lead poison report? On Jeremy Giesbrecht? Yes, here it is. It's. . . ."

I held my breath.

"Yes, it's negative," she answered in a business-like voice.

It was a difficult summer. Tim quit his interim job as a burglar alarm installer and worked full-time building Kids' Kottage Daycare Center, so we could complete the transition in the fall of 1981. I worked with our group family daycare home, took care of Jeremy and Charity, and in the evening helped Tim with the building. Often working till two or three in the morning we'd begin again the next morning at six-thirty a.m. It would have been a tough time even without a child with problems.

Jeremy continued to sleep spasmodically. During the hours he was awake he was often fussy. He made continual messes. We were exhausted mentally, physically, and emotionally. Spiritually we felt betrayed. Where was God? I felt I was hanging on to life by my fingernails.

One evening as Tim and I worked together installing the bathroom fixtures in the Kids' Kottage bathrooms, I remarked, "You know I feel as if I'll never be happy again. I don't mean that I'll never laugh again. We do that even now, but I feel like I'll never have that carefree, gutsy, all's well with the world, kind of happiness ever again."

Tim turned to look at me, his heavy eyebrows accenting the sadness in his brown eyes. "I know what you mean, Honey. If only we knew what's wrong with Jeremy. Maybe then it would be easier to bear."

5

The "Angel" Escaped

Tim and I transferred our membership to a larger church when we were expecting Charity. Trinity Church, not far from our home, became the focal point of not only our spiritual life but our social life as well.

We were quickly accepted into the Beta Sunday School class where we developed solid friendships. With the exception of Oak Hills Bible College, I had never made friends as quickly as at Trinity Church. Since most class members were approximately our age and many had young children, Mike Bortel, the associate pastor at the church and our Sunday school teacher, taught primarily marriage and family enrichment. Pastor Hart Christenson, the senior pastor, a humble godly man, communicated out of his own life's experience. Often he would say in a broken voice, "God is teaching me about being full of grace through my friend Dale who is paralyzed and confined to a wheelchair." Dean Palermo, our minister of music, designed the worship service to blend with the sermon.

In the Beta class we talked about the nitty gritty aspects of getting along with our spouse, teaching our children, and being a responsible worker. Then we came to worship to celebrate and pray and set goals for change. Trinity was just what we needed as we faced the question of what was wrong with Jeremy, as well as the larger question of where God and goodness figured into sin, evil, and the ordeal of suffering. One of the questions we asked ourselves was: Is having a mental handicap a result of the evil world or simply a more marked variation of intelligence? Jeremy, apart from his frustration at not being able to communicate, seemed relatively happy. I wondered if it was anymore of a gift to be highly intelligent, especially given the high suicide rate for gifted persons. As time went on and our knowledge of handicaps grew it became more and more evident to me that all of us are handicapped in some ways. Some find it difficult to work with numbers, others find it nearly impossible to accept love, while many people are paralyzed by fear of change. In God's eyes are these handicaps any less significant than legs that don't work or brains that function more slowly than others?

Marie Peterson, my teacher friend and a fellow member of the Beta class, and I often discussed these matters. I wondered what we would do without friends like Marie and her husband John, and others from Beta.

As in any group of human beings all of our experiences at church weren't perfect. Particularly as Jeremy began to regress, some people tried to put us on a shelf with a nice neat label. The mystery of Jeremy's regression touched us all. We first came to Trinity with a beautiful normal child; a year later there was no mistaking something was wrong. The fact that there was no diagnosis made it seem even more illusive and more difficult to accept. All of us who watched the old Jeremy slip away came a little closer to our own earthly mortality, our own lack of control, and it frightened each of us.

Most of those we knew at church were helpful. They would tell us about any new tests they thought we might try. They prayed for us. Most helpful of all were those who could accept Tim and me as people, not just "those parents of a regressing child."

For some friends accepting Jeremy as he was seemed to be more difficult. Angie, the mother of a child in Jeremy's Sunday school class cornered me one Sunday morning just before the Beta class began. "It's really not fair to the other children that Jeremy can walk around during story time and they have to sit still," she carped.

"His teachers haven't told us there was a problem," I answered. I could hear the surprise in my voice.

"They wouldn't say it," Angie pronounced, "but it doesn't seem fair that all the kids should suffer for one."

I could feel the heat in my face. I struggled for composure as I sought to find out what was behind Angie's outburst. "It isn't that Jeremy is naughty. He just can't focus long enough to sit still for an entire story. The teachers have told us he just wanders in the back of the room quietly humming, 'Jesus Loves Me,' and not bothering anyone."

"Well, my background is in education and I think . . . ." She paused, looking me straight in the eye. "I think kids like Jeremy should be with their own kind, not with normal kids who can sit still and learn."

Shame and rage filled me. I had been raised to look for good in everyone. My interpretation of that had often led me to believe if someone was not happy with me, it was because I had somehow failed them. However, at this moment I was more Jeremy's mother than a "people pleasing" child. It suddenly occurred to me that Jeremy's only chance for a near normal life was for Tim and me to stand up for him. After all, he could hardly talk now; he couldn't even speak for himself. With a chill in my voice I asked, "Angie, just how many handicapped children do you think there are in this church?"

Angie fidgeted in her chair. "Well, I don't know. I guess I really don't know if there are any others."

"And even if there were many others, Jeremy's problems are so unique he wouldn't fit into even an optimal classroom of handicapped children."

Angie started to reply when the lights flashed, a signal from Pastor Mike, our teacher, that the Beta class was about to begin.

Angie's continued gossip to others in church about Jeremy disrupting class didn't help our self-image as parents. Often her words would come back to us in escaped phrases from friends. Immediately they'd apologize, "I'm sorry. It just slipped out. I didn't want you to know she'd said that."

One day as a result of a family illness I babysat Angie's son. When she came to pick him up she stayed to chat a few minutes. During the conversation she said, "I've never understood why the government pays for preschool intervention programs anyway. Just because children are handicapped is no reason their parents should get a break." I stared at her. My mouth hung open.

"After all," she continued, "I pay to send my child to nursery school."

Taking my silence as encouragement she went on to tell me about how she had worked with Jeremy in the nursery.

Numbly I nodded acknowledgement as she droned on. "He took a cracker and I said, 'No, Jeremy.' He looked me right in the eye and ran away laughing. He knows what he's doing, Penny. He's fooling you and everybody else."

I felt as if Angie had pierced my soul.

Around the same time an older woman in our church stopped me, following choir one Sunday. "How's your boy?" she asked.

I explained to her how the testing so far was giving us no clues, but that we continued to be concerned about Jeremy's regression.

"We have a neighbor with a diabetic son who refused to take his insulin," she noted. "Ya' know, they put him in a foster home and in just a little while they got him to taking his insulin again. Now he's back home and doing fine."

Not comprehending the comparison I turned to go, smiled politely, and said, "That's wonderful. I'm glad it turned out so well for them."

This well-intentioned lady demanded, "Well, are you going to do it?"

"Do what?" I asked still bewildered.

"Put your boy in a foster home."

Finally, understanding the intent of her words I said with conviction, "No! We are not going to put Jeremy in a foster home. Even though we don't know what is wrong, we do know it's medical." I quoted Henry's oft repeated words, "Even if we were bad parents, and we're not, we could not have made Jeremy like he is." I paused, taking a deep breath. I had never defended myself so boldly. "If children could become like Jeremy from just bad parenting then the whole world would be filled with people who aren't normal—whatever normal is."

The woman sputtered, "Well, I just thought it might help for him to be placed. It sure helped my neighbor's boy."

The truth was that Jeremy wasn't the easiest child to care for in Sunday school. We knew that better than anyone. It was only through our determination to stay involved in church that we were able to to leave Jeremy at Sunday school We never knew for sure what he might do. It wasn't just his unpredictable behavior that concerned us but the fact that he was so active that he might get hurt or at the least break something in a kinetic frenzy.

Whenever we came to pick up Jeremy from his Sunday school class I would try to brace myself emotionally for what we might hear. One Sunday our good friends Karen and Mark Baden were teaching Jeremy's class. Mark said, "Wait till you hear this."

"We're sorry," Karen interrupted. "It happened so fast. I mean we just closed our eyes to pray before serving snack and . . ." I looked toward Jeremy as Karen spoke and could see a sticky orange color covering his white vest. ". . . And he just poured the pitcher of juice over his head!"

"He's gonna keep you young, Tim," Mark teased. "You'll have no time for middle-aged muscles to atrophy with Jeremy around."

Another time I picked Jeremy up from Sunday school while Tim went to get Charity from the baby nursery. Angie had substituted in the class room. I knew as soon as I saw her face that something had gone wrong.

"Penny," she said, "Jeremy ate several crayons today. I didn't catch him till it was too late."

"Don't worry about it, Angie. He's hard to keep up with. He eats them at home all the time. He has a strange craving for wax." I smiled hoping to ease her anxiety. "Besides crayons are non-toxic."

"I know that," Angie exclaimed. "I'm just worried that we won't have any crayons left."

I cried all the way home and the next Sunday brought new crayons to Jeremy's class. When I emptied the crayons from the carton into the nearly full crayon bucket I couldn't help but notice it was the size of a huge dishpan. In spite of my earlier remorse I laughed. Angie was wrong this time. It would take even Jeremy a long time to eat that many crayons.

Because our church was such an integral part of our lives it was often at the cutting edge of our journey to understand God and suffering. Why was Jeremy regressing? Some of the answers given to us from people within the church as well as from family members and friends were simplistic, some kindly misinformed, others similar to the answers I'd been given as a child. Many related to our parenting skills, still others to our spiritual condition. "God must be trying to teach you something." "God has picked you to raise a special child because you are such wonderful parents." "God is punishing you. He chastises those He loves." One of the most hurtful answers given to us regarding Jeremy's condition came from a person extremely close to us who believed Jeremy was demon-possessed.

Not everyone was calloused or insensitive to our hurt. Several friends from the Beta class encouraged us with a hug or just by their interest. Marie often called and simply offered a listening ear.

Although my friendship with Marie was not based on our crisis situation I was especially grateful for her support during this time in our lives. Kids' Kottage Daycare Center, now licensed by the State of Minnesota for twenty school-age children, still consumed a lot of my energy. Much work remained in the house addition above it, as well. Money was in short supply with our new venture especially because the recession hit that year of 1981. Many of our parents lost their jobs and therefore didn't need childcare anymore. It was good to have a close friend with whom to share both my triumphs and heartaches.

Our schedule was beginning to take a toll. Tim and I not only experienced physical fatigue, but were emotionally exhausted as well. Jeremy continued to be hyperactive, tearing his curtains off the wall, dumping out boxes of toys, running away, and sleeping only part of each night. Spiritually, we clung to the promise that God was with us. We begged God to protect Jeremy when we were just physically incapable of keeping up.

My mother, observing Jeremy's activity level and the continual need to chase after him. commented, "How can you stand it? You can't even go to the bathroom without worrying he'll get hurt."

We reminded her of our bargain with God. Indeed, it was congruent with our childhood belief system. "We'll do the very best we can to watch him and trust God to watch over and protect him from there."

One day Marie called after a particularly trying day with Jeremy and pressures of Kids' Kottage opening. "Penny," she said, "I wish there was something I could do. I'll never forget when our Erik was hospitalized with peri-orbital cellulitus (a severe eye infection) and you and Tim and Karen Baden came the first night with pop and magazines and rolls. I just wish I could do something concrete like that for you. I wish I could make it all better."

"Marie, you can't change things for Jeremy and neither can I, but you listen and that's what I need more than anything."

"Don't you wonder, Penny, why? I'm not even Jeremy's mother and I beg God to show me why Jeremy doesn't get better. When Erik got well we were so incredibly relieved, but it just doesn't seem fair that Jeremy can't be okay too. I get up to pray for Jeremy and you and Tim every morning at 5:30, but I don't know how to pray anymore."

"There you go, Marie. You just did something to help me in a concrete way. Tim and I are sometimes too tired to pray. Because Jeremy isn't better we need your prayers more than we'd ever need them if he was okay."

Christmas was coming, and in spite of everything, we made plans to celebrate Christ's birth with enthusiasm. Tim and I sang in the sanctuary choir. This year the cantata, "Love Came Down at Christmas," by John W. Peterson, was a healing balm to us each time we practiced it.

I also directed the Junior High Choir, "Free Spirit." I was pleased with the voice quality and musical knowledge of the group. More than that, I had shared with them our concerns for Jeremy and was touched by the empathy they showed at their innocent age. Many of the kids took a special interest in Jeremy and Charity. I loved them for it.

The night of the Christmas pageant finally came. I was nervous as I directed Free Spirit to line up. When it was our turn the kids sang beautifully and were rewarded by the enthusiastic applause of the audience. Twenty-five junior highers smiled knowing they'd done well.

I was "riding high" as I rushed to the back of the church, slipped my robe on and sprinted up the balcony stairs to join the rest of the senior choir. Jeremy's Cherub Choir was next on the program and I didn't want to miss a bit of it.

The Cherubs were made up of about twenty, three-to five-year-olds. I hoped Jeremy would be standing close to a teacher. I had forgotten to give her last minute advice since I'd been busy before the concert practicing with Free Spirit.

Reaching the top of the stairs, I heard laughter echoing in the sanctuary. I looked down over the crowd of six hundred to the platform. As if posing for a Christmas card the blonde, blue-eyed youngsters draped in robes of white, were peering over the huge red bows hugging their necks. I marveled at the angelic scene before me, but was startled to notice my little blonde angel creeping from out of the "Christmas card" ever so stealthily to the riser's edge. Reaching the end Jeremy jumped off and pranced to the baptistry. *Oh, God! Don't let there be water in it. He'll jump in.* Jeremy loved water. The baptistry must have been empty because with hardly a sideways glance he was off again, running toward the piano this time. Then back through the choir loft. As if mesmerized, I watched. My throat was constricted. My eyes burned. Again and again Jeremy eluded first the clutch of the music director, then the desperate grasp of his teacher.

As the chase progressed I noticed that Jeremy seemed oblivious to those resolutely trying to capture him. I knew his peripheral vision was excellent and that he could see his pursuers without even looking their way. Just as they grabbed for him he'd spin around and instantly whirl away.

The laughter that had rippled across the auditorium minutes before had now become a roar. *Dear God! Don't they know he can't help it?*

I heard Tim's voice, hoarse with emotion, behind me. "Penny, do something."

In my hysteria, I too was laughing. Barely able to make out the words, I whispered loudly, "What do you want me to do? Fly down there?" I saw intense pain in Tim's eyes. I looked at him feeling my own pain so intensely my stomach ached. We connected almost like an electric current; each feeling the other's hurt . . . but still . . . I laughed. Tears pushed to be released. I couldn't let them out. I couldn't let go.

As the Cherub Choir finished their third song Jeremy was finally retrieved behind the Christmas tree by the music director.

Angie glared at me. "What kind of a mother are you?" her eyes accused. I wondered if the anger registered in her eyes was because of her disappointment that no one had been able to hear her son sing over the laughter, or seemed to notice his perfect behavior during the recital.

As our senior choir sang, Love Came Down at Christmas, tears trickled down my cheeks. *Oh, dear God come down to me now. I need you! I need you!*

I searched for Tim after the concert. I looked in the choir room and in the church foyer, but he was nowhere to be found. A friend of mine remarked kindly, "Don't worry about Jeremy tonight, Penny. People loved it. When Mindy was three she spent the whole performance with her dress over her head. I lived to tell about it, and you will too."

I laughed in spite of the intense emotion I was feeling. "Tim, over here," I called, seeing him emerge from the choir bathroom. His eyes were red and puffy. "Honey, are you okay?" I had only seen Tim cry twice before. The first time when discussing a breakup while dating, the next at Jeremy's birth.

Tim's voice was broken, "It just got to me tonight. They were laughing at Jeremy."

"Tim, hardly anyone at church knew there was anything wrong. They just thought it was cute. I laughed too."

"I've hoped all along we'd find out how to help Jeremy. That it wouldn't be serious. When we were singing the cantata about Jesus coming down at Christmas. I just wondered why? Why is this happening? What does God want with us?

"Oh, Tim!" I put my arms around him not caring who saw me.

"Penny, I know now. Jeremy wouldn't have done that unless . . . unless something was really wrong."

6

Autistic?

Jeremy started school at the North Suburban Day Activity Center at the end of August 1981. He was three-and-a-half years old. The first day the mini-bus pulled into our driveway to pick him up my stomach twisted. Gently I pushed my little blonde son up the stairs of the bus. I found it hard to accept that Jeremy needed to go to school now. It wasn't that I was opposed to preschool. Jeremy had been scheduled to attend our church's nursery school program until the testing at Children's Hospital indicated a need for a more intensive program. I just didn't want to send him to "this kind of a school."

The bus driver, a pretty young woman of about twenty, smiled brightly, "Hi! I'm Wendy. I'll be Jeremy's bus driver." She seemed bright and cheerful; I hoped she was a good driver. As the bus pulled out of our driveway I waved to Jeremy through tear filled eyes.

Returning to the house, I was surprised that my reluctance was mixed with a sense of relief. For the first time in months, Jeremy's safety was not my sole responsibility. For three hours, every day, I wouldn't have to worry about where Jeremy was at every moment. Shaking my head, I walked back inside, confused by the ambivalence of my feelings.

Jeremy seemed to enjoy the bus ride to the Day Activity Center (DAC). The reports from school sounded positive and we liked his vivacious and talented teacher. Early in the fall Jeremy learned to ride a trike. His skills at maneuvering around the more severely handicapped children in the gym would have been amazing, even for a normal three-and-a-half-year-old.

I began attending the "mom's group" which met every other week at one of the homes of mothers of the children in the DAC. I was nervous about it right from the start. Their children were retarded. What would I have in common with them? Even the director of the DAC had said that Jeremy would start Early Intervention, in the Moundsview School District, in the fall of '82 and then probably go to Kindergarten the following year.

At the first meeting, I was shocked at how intelligent and "normal" these mothers seemed. Frequently the conversation turned to the educational future of our children. Every mother dreamed of her child advancing to the Mounds View School District's mainstreaming program—a program where children with special needs attend school with "normal" children receiving extra help from an aide or special teacher. I felt guilty knowing almost certainly that this was where Jeremy was headed. At my first "mom's meeting," one of the mother's asked me who Jeremy's teacher was.

"Sharon," I replied.

"Oh, Jeremy's in the highest group then. My son was in that group last year, but then they decided it was too advanced for him." She paused and added with a sad smile, "When I was a teacher I always thought how terrible it would be to have your child flunk a grade at school. But when your child flunks retarded school that's really bad."

"I'm sorry, that must have been really hard for you." I was touched by her candor.

"I cried buckets then, but I'm kinda over it now. What can you do?"

"What can you do?" kind of characterized much of our conversation. What can you do when families won't accept your child's handicap? What can you do when there isn't an appropriate Sunday school class at church? What can you do when you can't get a babysitter to sit for your handicapped child?

What can you do, but go on? One of those times of "going on," in spite of the way society coped with Jeremy, was when we decided to have our family portrait taken.

Family pictures were important to me. Even though our budget was extremely tight I joined a family plan for photographs. The night of our appointment, we rushed to get everyone "picture ready" and make it to the studio on time. We needn't have bothered for when we entered the waiting area it was packed with people. Tim and I took turns walking the short hallway with

Jeremy while Charity, in characteristic fashion, played quietly with toys. Finally, over an hour after our scheduled appointment, our name was called. Giving the children's hair one final brushing we walked in and positioned ourselves as the young photographer instructed.

"Smile," he said brightly. WE SMILED.

"Smile!" he repeated still not clicking the camera shutter.

He locked eyes with Jeremy and spat tersely, "What's wrong with you? Look at your baby sister, she smiles better than you. Now, SMILE this time."

Tim touched Jeremy gently, "Come on Honey, smile."

"Hmmm. Stubborn isn't he?"

I felt tired of fighting but I'd taken as much as I could handle. "Look, Jeremy is in diagnostic treatment right now. He doesn't understand what you mean."

"Oh," the photographer replied defensively, "I thought there was something wrong with him."

I cocked my head toward him. "I work with children every day and many children without learning difficulties might not react any differently than Jeremy has tonight." My voice softened. "Are you new at this business?"

"Yeah, I am."

"Let me give you some advice. If you treat children with respect, the same respect you'd like to be treated with, you'll get many more smiles from them."

The pictures turned out just fine.

By the beginning of November the notes from school became less positive. Jeremy was switched to a lower group. He had "flunked retarded school."

Two weeks later we were called to a meeting with Henry Panowitsch and the professionals from the Day Activity Center. The report was discouraging. One test measuring Jeremy's communication abilities placed him at a developmental age of eight months.

"Eight months!" I blurted. "Are you sure you have that right. He still talks at home." Jane, the speech therapist, nodded sadly. "Yes, I know. Sharon told me he talks at home, but at school he rarely says anything."

Sadly I acknowledged, "His speech at home has regressed, too, I guess."

Henry again stepped in to lighten this most recent blow, "Penny, the issue is not which month Jeremy's development is at or what label we can give him. That isn't really useful. The issue is how can we help this young man and get some sense of what is going on in his mind?"

I noticed again how respectfully Henry spoke of my child and my soul thanked him. I listened carefully as he continued. "There is a woman at Children's Hospital who is the best I've seen to get an idea of how to work with children like Jeremy. She's helped many children in the District when we just weren't sure where they fit."

Cheryl, Jeremy's new teacher, interrupted, "Do you mean Sheila Merzer?"

"Yes, if that's agreeable to Tim and Penny. I'd like to call her today and set up a time when all of us could meet with her down at Minneapolis Children's Hospital." Henry turned to me. "Penny, I think you'll like Sheila. She has an uncanny sense about her for figuring ways of understanding these kids who don't fit into our neat boxes."

We agreed, trusting Henry's instincts and his obvious concern for Jeremy. He had certainly shown himself worthy of that trust in the months we had known him. Henry's insistence that we accept that Jeremy's condition was not our fault, gave us encouragement to keep going. Even though a part of us knew we were good parents there was another part asking, "What did we do wrong?" I went over and over my pregnancy. "Was it something I was exposed to when I was pregnant? Did I drink too much milk? Maybe it was the time I lifted the sewing machine from the closet and pulled a muscle." Tim had his own thoughts although his quiet personality made it more difficult for him to verbalize his fears. Tim's main fear was that Jeremy's condition was genetic and that he carried the gene since he had some mentally handicapped cousins. Some of the questions we shared were related to the spiritual dimension: "Did God need to teach us a lesson?" "Were we being punished through our son's problems?" "Had our imperfect parenting caused his regression?" Needless to say, Henry's constant reminders that it wasn't our fault were like a balm to a deep wound.

Both Tim and I felt optimistic about having Jeremy evaluated again. We remained convinced that somehow we would solve the puzzle of Jeremy's regression. Sheila sounded as if she might be able to provide at least one of the missing pieces.

I arrived at the address given us, proud that I had found it without getting lost. I was surprised by the humble appearance of the old home now converted to facilitate The Program for Autistic and Other Exceptional Children run by the Minneapolis Children's Hospital. The old porch which served as a makeshift foyer had a crooked floor. Inside, the receptionist area was cheerfully decorated although obviously cramped for space.

I was the first to arrive. Sheila Merzer was much younger than I'd expected her to be. Her long black hair flowed midway down her back and her face was friendly and warm. I liked and trusted her immediately. Henry, representing the Mounds View School District, arrived next and greeted me with a huge bear hug. "Hi, Penny! How are you?" I knew he really wanted to know.

Jeremy's evaluation began with games and teacher-child interaction. I could see that Jeremy was doing well. I smiled. Surely they'd be impressed. As we watched from behind the one-way glass the video-taping of the interaction, I noticed Sheila intently studying my face. What was she looking for?

Sheila and Lyle Chastain, co-directors of this marvelous program, felt Jeremy would fit into their program nicely. The cost was high, but she and Henry bargained together and easily resolved the financial arrangements. I agreed that Tim and I would drive Jeremy between home and school each day to alleviate the expense of busing by the Mounds View School District.

The day I took Jeremy to Sheila and Lyle's program was the first time anyone had ever used the word autistic in a way that connected the term with Jeremy. Although he was still essentially undiagnosed, autistic-like was the word they used to describe Jeremy's behavior.

Tim and I read everything we could find about autism, which we understood to be really a label for describing communication disorders. Much of the information terrified us. We read of autistic children who were locked in their rooms, children who bit family members, pulled hair, or abused themselves. In one school in the south, cattle prods were being used to electrically shock children into obedience. The school defended their treatment by claiming there was no hope of education, so they trained the children as if they were animals.

Images of one story I read during this time haunted me for many months after. An exhausted and severely depressed father found the difficult life he and his wife faced with their autistic youngster impossible to bear any longer. One day he came home from work, went to his son's room, and pulled out a loaded revolver. His son felt the shiny new object. The father pulled the trigger, killing his son.

Some of the information we received about autism came from

people we knew who had had some experience with the disorder. One evening we were at a church dinner with our family. A woman I had seen at church only occasionally observed Jeremy and then asked pointedly, "What is wrong with your son?"

I explained that we didn't know what had happened but for lack of a better term described him as autistic-like.

She clucked her tongue sympathetically. "My friends had an autistic daughter."

"How is she doing?" I asked hardly wanting to know.

"Oh they put her in an institution. They had to lock her in her room all day and it was just getting to be too much."

I felt hot as I struggled to get some air. "How sad."

Nonchalantly she replied, "Oh no, not at all. They have four beautiful normal daughters and they're all doing great."

Occasionally, we heard stories of autistic adults who lived with their parents and enjoyed fairly normal lives. One article I read stated that ten percent of autistic people are savants or geniuses in some area—a much higher percentage than in the normal population.

While we waited everyday for Jeremy at Sheila and Lyle's building we had time to bombard the staff with questions about autism. They warned us to be careful of giving too much credence to what we read. "Much of what's available was written before autistic children were intervened with as preschoolers," Sheila reminded us. "We don't have the statistics in yet on how much difference that will make, but we think there will be a huge distinction."

One article that helped us more clearly define autism in our early searching was written by Sheila Merzer and Lyle Chastain and entitled, "Social Skills: Assessment and Interventions." The article described individual children showing the common thread of communication, behavior, and sometimes cognitive disorders connecting an otherwise very diverse group.

Sheila and Lyle described the largest group of children diagnosed at their program this way: "While the failure to develop communicative language is generally perceived by most parents as the primary handicap of their young autistic child, a closer look at the autistic toddler generally reveals a child whose functioning is atypical in a wide variety of ways. Hyperactive and easily distracted or lethargic and difficult to motivate, the child is generally unresponsive to his parents' efforts to manage his behavior."

Cindy Nollette, the counselor of the team at the Autism Program, spent at least one hour a week with either Tim or me talking about Jeremy and how we were coping.

We continued to hang on to our belief that Jeremy was not autistic. Surely, someday he would be normal. After all, God could heal him. After all, we were good parents; together we had an edge on other families. After all, hadn't God always blessed our families with good health? We would make the difference! We took much comfort in the fact that Jeremy was not typically autistic, remaining confident we would eventually find a cure. We were willing to do our part. Surely God would do His.

Cindy, in a gentle but persistent way, encouraged us to see that Jeremy was very hurt and would perhaps never get much better. Sometimes we'd wonder, *What do they want us to do? Give up?*

We felt like we were doing battle. On one side were the articles and stories of kids who supposedly overcame their handicaps because of their parent's perseverance, and on the other professionals insisting, "Look this is what's happening. You have to face reality."

At times I felt like screaming, *Don't you think we know what reality is? Who do you think cleans the Vaseline Jeremy rubs all over the walls, and bedding and toys? Who gets up with Jeremy in the middle of the night as he giggles and kicks and runs and never settles down? Who runs to find him when he escapes through a door or a window?*

I think we knew the reality of Jeremy's problems, but we weren't yet ready to accept the permanence of the condition.

In my journal on January 31, 1982 I wrote, *I feel like we're preparing for a race, but no one has told us whether we'll be competing in the 50-yard dash or the 20-mile marathon.*

Shortly after Jeremy was enrolled in Sheila's program we were told about mega-vitamin therapy. Dr. Bernhard Remler had had some success with it in California. Grasping for any hope available, we threw ourselves into the plan taking Jeremy off all sugar, preservatives, and dyes as the plan indicated. We also began giving him huge doses of vitamins twice a day.

For thirty minutes each day I divided the pills into correct quantities, mashing them together with a meat hammer. The most difficult part of our assignment was preparing something that would disguise the strong taste of Vitamin B-12. The regimen also meant a big change in our life style. We couldn't eat at church or with friends in their homes.

A week after Jeremy had begun mega-vitamin therapy he seemed calmer. One night he said clearly, "I want some candy!"

We called my parents hoping desperately he would repeat the coveted words, but he didn't. In fact, he never repeated them.

We asked Sheila, "Do you think it's working? Do you think it's a good sign that Jeremy talked?"

Sheila reminded us, "Kids like Jeremy sometimes say or do something almost unbelievable, but it's not uncommon for it never to be repeated again. It's just too early to tell."

Jeremy remained on the diet for about three months with little or no improvement. The fight to get him to take the vitamins became overwhelming and Jeremy won. Finally we reasoned that even though the lack of sugar may have calmed him some, the effort and change in our lifestyle to accommodate his diet was too great a price for the small return. Several people encouraged us to check into hypoglycemia as a possible cause for Jeremy's autistic-like behavior. Some said they knew of adults and children who had been severely altered by the hypoglycemic condition. We were pleased when Dr. Reno Backus, the pediatric neurologist associated with the Minneapolis Children's Hospital's autism program, agreed to test for it. The test involved blood samplings drawn several times over approximately a four hour span. Jeremy and I arrived at Minneapolis Children's Hospital laden with books, toys and treats to help pass the time between the tests.

Jeremy went willingly to the lab for the first blood to be drawn from his arm. When the needle pricked him he stared up at me, his hazel eyes pleading for protection. Each time we returned to the lab, I fought the impulse to take him and run. But where could we go? Could I ever take him so far that he wouldn't be frustrated, that we wouldn't have to deal with society's nuances? As I helped to hold him down, I bit my lip hard. I shoved my tears back and tried to be tough. In my heart I knew it was the only way I could ever help him.

We waited anxiously for the results of the test. Again we were told, "The test is negative."

The days passed during the initial six-week trial session in The Program for Autistic and Other Exceptional Children. We asked permission to keep Jeremy in the program part time through the end of May so that he wouldn't have to get used to a third school. Our request was approved partly because Sheila and Lyle didn't feel they had a strategy ready to send with him to another school.

We weren't as optimistic about Jeremy's prognosis as when he began the program, but we continued to be impressed by the way Sheila and her staff worked with these "exceptional" kids.

Their methodology included finding Jeremy's interests, such as food, music, trucks, and bubbles, and then using those to teach him concepts that would be a foundation for communication.

One day Dr. Backus came to do a neurological exam of Jeremy at the school. He laughed as Jeremy felt of his face and stethoscope. "I have yet to examine one of these kiddies. But they never fail to examine me."

"Dr. Backus," Tim asked, "What is the prognosis for Jeremy?"

"Frankly, I worry about these kiddies. Some of them get worse. They keep regressing. Some get some better, but are still basically autistic-like and then a few seem to snap out of it."

"Do you think something metabolic causes autism?" Tim pressed.

"I think it may be metabolic or possibly physiological in origin. I wish I was young enough to figure out the mystery of autism. It's going to take some young doctor, someone who's willing to work for years without much reward to find out more about autism." He patted Jeremy on the head. "He's a beautiful boy. I'd trade him for four teenagers any day."

In the early spring of 1982 I attended a Women's Day Away at church. Much time was allowed for prayer and journaling. We were asked to journal our thoughts to Jesus as if He just came one day and sat next to us in our car available for a long talk. I wrote: *Jesus, you're here! What are you doing in my car? Are we in heaven? Where do you want me to go? Why haven't you healed Jeremy? What is wrong with him? How can we help him? Do you love us when we hurt so bad? Why is life so hard? Oh dear Jesus, I have so many questions. so few answers . . . .*

Jesus, why don't you just come down from heaven, instead of being so austere . . . . Don't you know how we need you? Why can't our heartache be short like Marie's when Erik got well in just ten days. Lord, you say, 'Ask what you will, and it will be done for you.' Well, I'm here, and I'm asking for Jeremy to be healed.

Sometimes, I wonder how Christian I really am when my doubts begin to surface. I feel like I'm in a deep, dark tunnel. Be patient with my doubting. I want to believe, Lord. Help me to be still, to learn, and to be sensitive to the needs of others.

A few days later Jeremy talked. He said, "Jesus Loves Me, Bible Tells Me, Mom, Pen Pen Pen, Run, Run, Run, Happy Birthday."

It seemed a miracle! We told our friends. They cried.

That night Jeremy drank a half bottle of Robitussin. We called poison control—again. They said he'd sleep it off. The next day he had a hangover.

God, why is it so much easier to
  write to you what I feel.
So often, I can't pray.
  How to do it?
Shall I pray believing
  we should be exempt from pain?
Shall I pray that our son's silence,
  the hurt and anger we feel at
  life should somehow glorify you?
Shall I pray that we won't lose our faith, or that other's won't
  because you've "allowed this?"
Shall I pray with hope, for a future that
  looks bleak and cruel?
Shall I pray to love those who pious though they be, slander
our
  son who cannot raise one word against them?
Shall I pray for a forgiving spirit for those who look down on
us
  who hurt us deep in our innermost part?
Shall I pray for forgiveness of blasphemy for my anger to
You—
  for being audacious enough to be honest about it?
Oh Lord!
My spirit knows not . . . how to pray.
Make intercession for me.
I believe! Help thou my unbelief!

7

The Healing Service

Here we go again, I thought as I sat down at the child size table with Henry, Sheila, Lyle and the DAC staff for the final evaluation of Jeremy's progress while in the Autism Program. Tim had stayed home with Charity and the kindergarten children at Kids' Kottage. I wished he were with me now.

"Jeremy is four now, Penny." Sheila began. "He's been in the program for six months and we really have seen no improvement." Sheila tossed her long black hair over her shoulder, eyeing me intently. *Aha! she's watching for my reaction again.* Sheila was intensively sensitive to how much we were ready to hear. Today, what I heard seemed too much. The past six months had been painful. We had faced the fact that Jeremy was autistic-like. Now Sheila said he wasn't improving. Even autistic children are supposed to improve.

Sheila gently interrupted my thoughts. "Penny, we have tried at least twenty intervention strategies for Jeremy in the past six months. Each time, Jeremy does something six steps beyond the task we are trying to teach him. Then, sometimes for weeks he will not attend to even the simplest activity."

"Don't autistic children normally learn, though perhaps more slowly, Sheila?" I asked.

"Jeremy is just not typically autistic. Although 'autistic' is a wastebasket expression for all kinds of communication disorders and there are many probable causes and results, Jeremy just doesn't fit the general pattern we've seen here. He is different."

Henry added, "I've worked in preschool intervention for many years at Mounds View School District and I did my doctoral training at Mayo Clinic, but I have never met a more mysterious young man than Jeremy."

As always, Henry spoke respectfully of our son. He really saw value in all human life, handicapped or not. Tim and I trusted people like Henry, Lyle, and Sheila. They had become important support to us as we grieved for the normal Jeremy we once had, and learned to love and accept this little boy who took his place. Indeed, it seemed the Jeremy we once knew had died and there had never been a funeral.

Henry and Sheila discussed what the next step should be for Jeremy. The consensus seemed to be, "Let's wait for future clues from Jeremy's own development to help us decide about the future."

In the end, we decided to keep Jeremy in the summer autism program, but have a live-in summer tutor Tim and I had privately hired go with him and be his teacher. Sheila and Lyle agreed that if we provided the teacher, they would train her plus Jeremy could go to the school without charge. Henry even offered busing from the school district. I chuckled as I watched Henry and Sheila good-naturedly bargain. We kidded Sheila about her fund raising skills. "You should be a politician, Sheila," I teased her once as I watched her maneuver a deal for Jeremy.

"Forget that," Tim argued, "We need her here."

I realized again how fortunate we were to have two people like Henry and Sheila helping Jeremy. Helping us. Even though they were extremely busy they always took time to inquire about how Tim and I were coping.

My mind came quickly back to the present when I heard Sheila mention Bakerstown.

"Bakerstown?" Do they have a program for autistic children there?" I asked.

"Oh yes," Sheila assured me, "They have many of our kids and do a great job."

My heart beat faster, and my throat felt tight. *Not Bakerstown!* It was the school the mother's group at the DAC had talked about. I remembered my friend's pain filled words, "When your child flunks retarded school that's bad."

I looked questioningly at Henry. "Didn't you say Jeremy would be in the Mounds View Early Intervention Program when he was four? I thought all of these schools"—I spread my arms indicating the diagnostic classroom we sat in—"were just a stopgap measure till Jeremy was old enough to go to a program in his own school district."

Henry's brow furrowed as he answered. "Penny, I'm sorry if you misunderstood. The Mounds View Program is designed for kids who will be mainstreamed into the regular classes. A year ago Jeremy wasn't that far behind. But, now it doesn't seem to me he would be ready for—" He cleared his throat. "You seem reluctant to send him to Bakerstown? Is there a reason?"

"When Jeremy went to the DAC the mothers there used to talk about Bakerstown. No one wanted their kids to go there. I got the impression Bakerstown is the end of the line."

"Penny, I think Bakerstown is a very good school for the right child. Labels are useless at this point. What we have to decide is this, where is the functioning level of the child? Then we try to match the child with the level of functioning of other children in a group situation."

Silently I wondered, *What would have happened to Helen Keller if the only consideration had been her level of functioning? What kind of a school would they have put her in?*

"Look, we don't have to decide right now. I'll tell you what. Let's do this thing." In spite of my distress, I smiled at Henry's typical German verbiage. "Why don't you and Tim and I go take a look at Bakerstown and if you want to see the Mounds View Program we can look at that too. If you think Jeremy might fit in by fall, then we can talk about that, but I believe you'll see that The Early Intervention Program, is what you'd want for Jeremy, someday too, if he were to get better."

I gulped. I knew Henry was right. I had to face the fact that at least for now Jeremy was not making progress.

"There are many options to look at. I'm sure we can find one you'll feel good about."

As the meeting concluded Henry gave Sheila a friendly hug. "You know you're a tough lady to bargain with, but that's okay because you do it for all the right reasons."

Henry touched my arm. "How do you feel about everything today? Are you doing okay?"

I gave him a tired smile. "Henry, Tim and I both trust you and Sheila. We'll go with you to look at Bakerstown and then we'll see."

Henry, Tim, and I took the country road to Bakerstown on a beautiful spring day in April. Tim and I had made arrangements for Charity's care. Jeremy and all the children from Kids' Kottage Daycare Center were safely at school.

We arrived for the interview right on schedule. Manya Thompson introduced herself as the due process administrator. Lyle, representing The Program for Autistic and Other Exceptional Children, was already there. Manya seemed to know Henry well. She immediately reminded him of some paper work she wanted mailed to her. The third time she mentioned it he turned to us and rolled his eyes, but to her he said, "Yes, I'll see that you get it immediately."

Manya was professional, if not business-like, as she led us briskly through classrooms of fairly high-functioning children. "Is this where Jeremy would be if he came here?" I asked Manya.

"No, I'll show you that room last," she said.

We wove in and out of classrooms briefly greeting the teachers and then quickly moving to the next room. My heart went out to these kids. A young Downs child tugged on my skirt. "Hi! How you?"

"I'm fine, Dear. How are you?" I patted her blonde head. I noticed my discomfort with mentally handicapped people was gone. I first thought it was because of Jeremy, but then later thought it more likely that I never before had been exposed to handicapped people. It occurred to me again that all of us are handicapped in some way, just in varying degrees.

The tour was nearly finished. "We have one room left," Manya announced, stopping before the closed door. This would be the room where Jeremy would be placed. As Manya opened the door a beautiful blonde teacher came forward introducing herself as Gail. I was only momentarily distracted by her beauty. I reached for Tim's hand. The stench of human excrement filled my nostrils. Three children to my right sat tied in potty chairs squealing unintelligible sounds. In front of me, a young girl hung from a wooden frame, eyes rolling back into her head. A little girl with a tiny head clung to my skirt.

"This is where Jeremy will be," Manya announced matter-of-factly.

There had to be a mistake! Jeremy was beautiful. He didn't belong with these children. The room swam before me. Feeling my cheeks grow hot I concentrated on holding back the gag struggling to erupt from my throat. In panic I searched for a door, but remembered I had no idea where the rest rooms were. In the blur I heard the surprise in Lyle's voice as she asked, "Is this the most appropriate placement for Jeremy?"

Tim's hand felt sweaty in mine. He squeezed it tightly.

"Sheila told me Jeremy functions like an infant," Manya said bluntly.

"In some ways he is very different from this population of kids." Lyle spoke carefully.

Henry, too, seemed concerned, "What would you say is the potential of these young people?"

Manya answered casually. "Their potential is zero. They are so low functioning their goals are baseline."

Suddenly I came back to reality. My initial revulsion turned to rage. These weren't my kids. No human being has zero potential. The adrenaline flowing through me gave me the courage to walk, to smile, and thank the beautiful teacher. Finally with heavy legs we reached Henry's car.

When we arrived home and were finally alone, I said to Tim, "Jeremy will go to Bakerstown over my dead body."

Henry agreed to help us find an alternative program after our negative experience at Bakerstown. We visited the The Communication Interaction Disorders (CID) classroom together. Carrie, a young energetic woman who would be Jeremy's teacher, pranced around her fellow teachers showing off Jeremy's picture, "Isn't he cute?"

"I'll take him," another chimed in. Here were people who would value our son as we did. People who could see his potential. After all, we still didn't know what was wrong with him. Maybe we could still find the "miracle cure."

With much hope for Jeremy's fall program we began a summer full of optimism for the future. Carole, the girl we had hired to tutor Jeremy, was a social science major at Bethel College. With thick black hair that flowed to her waist and casual jean attire, she looked like a throw back to the 60's. Many of the applicants for the job had been impressive, but when Carole came we sensed a quiet maturity. We knew she was the one we wanted to work with Jeremy.

Carole and Jeremy spent every morning at the Autism Program where Carole tried many new intervention techniques. Afternoons, she taught Jeremy to swim in our pool. Often we'd see him on Carole's back and hear his sweet voice, "Jesus loves me, this I know," as he filled his fists with her lovely thick hair.

Carole kept a journal as part of her communication with the staff at the Autism Program. On her last day she wrote:

I've grown so attached to Jeremy. I almost wish he was a classic autistic child so this type of tutoring [would have] glorious results, but I've had a right feeling this summer about spending intense one-to-one time with him and doing the best I can; I think he does need this even though we can't see obvious success.

Tim and I were finally able to accept the fact that Jeremy was autistic-like. But we found it more difficult to accept that Jeremy wasn't learning even as well as typical autistic children.

Two-year-old Charity, however, provided comic relief for all of us. She also made it her business to keep everyone on schedule, reminding us where we should be, when we should be there and what we should bring along. Often as we left the house she would say, "Daddy, do you have the checkbook?"

One Saturday night I laid out her clothes for Sunday school. "Mommy," she said matter-of-factly, "I don't want to wear that dress to Sunday 'Kool tomorrow."

"What will we do when she's sixteen, Tim?" I asked laughing.

Charity was also a very sensitive child. Already she seemed to be Jeremy's best teacher. She could get response from him in laughter and play as none of the rest of us could. Often they played chase around the house or in the daycare center. Jeremy ran faster than Charity, but he'd wait till she was close behind and then run giggling off again. Sometimes he would even turn and chase her.

Shortly after Charity's second birthday, we decided that any kid who could tell us what she was wearing to "Sunday 'Kool" could also be one less kid to diaper. Since Jeremy was still not potty-trained and had outgrown cloth diapers we used disposable for both of our children. Our disposable diaper bill was competing for space in our limited budget. Highly motivated, we began to encourage training with pretty "big girl panties" and special treats.

I explained to Charity in great detail how she could accomplish this new task. After hearing the same speech several times she looked at me with her Brooke Shields' eyes and declared, "Mommy, don't talk to me about that *anymore*."

We welcomed Charity's animation as a welcome relief from the stress we often felt while dealing with Jeremy's unpredictability.

Indeed, it was often difficult for friends and family to accept the fact that he was handicapped because, "He looks so normal." They often told us, "I bet he's just fooling you; someday he'll just start talking," or "Have you tried spanking?"

We had tried spanking. When Jeremy's regression and hyperactivity were first noticed we felt insecure about our parenting skills. We thought, *We* must be doing something wrong. Maybe we love him so much we've spoiled him.

Friends had not only encouraged us to spank him "with a spoon," but, while guests in our home, had spanked him themselves. They tried to model for us how good parents get their children to stay in bed. Even though the spanking was not excessively hard, it had obviously been inappropriate for Jeremy who had no idea why he needed to stay in bed when his little muscles screamed to move. When the question, "Have you tried spanking?" came up I felt shame as I acknowledged the sad fact that we had, indeed, tried spanking.

Although we understood people meant well their remarks cut deeply. They goaded that place deep within making us wonder, *Have we done something to deserve this, God?*

Tim's parents and sisters from Canada visited us that summer. They believed Jeremy would be healed if we had a healing service for him. Tim and I, who had spent so much of our lives dealing with Jeremy and his mysterious handicap, wanted to believe more than anyone that Jeremy would be healed. If anyone has faith to believe their child will be well, it is parents. Indeed, it had taken months for us to finally accept that what had happened to Jeremy was not just a minor learning disability, soon to be overcome. Our faith that nothing bad would happen to us if we trusted God and prayed for our son, which we had done daily since his conception, finally had come face to face with the reality that Jeremy was not improving, but becoming worse.

Faith hadn't been a problem. Accepting what was happening to Jeremy had been another matter.

It was becoming difficult for us to believe that God could heal in this age and yet for some reason choose not to. We knew firsthand now, the taste of suffering. Also, unlike our family and friends, we were surrounded by new acquaintances from the schools Jeremy had attended and the hospitals and clinics where he was tested. Not only had they failed to experience divine healing, many had also divorced as a result of the strain of the condition of their children. Contrary to what some thought, we learned that the divorce rate is high among parents of handicapped children. Other children we heard about had been removed from their natural homes as a result of physical abuse or neglect. We could no longer believe that "God chose special parents to care for handicapped children." The parents we met in support groups came from all professions, in all different shapes and sizes, and from a variety of economic groups and family systems.

If God did heal in this age, we wondered if He would choose to heal Jeremy. After all, at least Jeremy had a home where people loved him. Many of the children we knew hadn't even that.

We shared these feelings during the visit with Tim's family. They attended a church where praying for healing was a common occurrence and felt concern over our searching for answers that fit the "world situation" we saw around us.

We understood the anxiety that filled the hearts of Tim's family. They wanted Jeremy to be normal because they loved us and had some sense of what we were going through. Jeremy's handicap ran against their belief, "If you have faith, God will bless you with good health and safety."

Tim wrote to his parents after they'd returned to Canada, *"Just because we are Christians does not mean we are immune to illness. We have to face the fact that Jeremy may never get better. Even though Jeremy isn't normal he is a sweet boy and we love him very much just as he is."*

Tim and I, in private, however, continued to wrestle with the Biblical question of healing.

At Oak Hills Bible College we had learned that Jesus' healings were to show Himself to be God. The apostles who didn't have the Bible in written form as we do today also needed a sign to show God's power in their age. Yet, we wondered, what if we're mistaken? What if healing is for today? What about the verse in James 5:14ff? I remembered it well, "Is any among you sick. Let him call the elders of the church, and let them pray over him, anointing with oil in the name of the Lord; and the prayer offered in faith will restore the one who is sick, and the Lord will raise him up, and if he has committed sins, they will be forgiven him."

We hung painfully over a great chasm. On one side we heard Bible verses like Matthew 7:7, "Ask, and it shall be given to you; seek and you shall find; knock, and it shall be opened unto you."

On the other, we heard the cries of millions of innocent children starving to death, Christian people claiming healing yet dying of cancer, and our own Jeremy mysteriously regressing. God was certainly not intervening to change such circumstances, at least not for the great majority.

Both Tim and I were exhausted, emotionally, physically, and spiritually. We had followed every medical lead. We had done all we knew. Our spirits were weary after two grueling years of unanswered questions. But finally we decided to give God the opportunity to heal Jeremy and glorify Himself if He chose to.

And so it happened in July of 1982 that we gathered.

The day was bright and balmy. A gentle breeze flicked the leaves in the sun. Under the trees we gathered. Quietly. Sweet love enfolding us with expectancy.

One by one we came together—until the circle was complete.

Pastor Hart softly reminded us why we were meeting. All eyes were turned to our little son.

"Lord, here we are," our pastor prayed, "asking you for healing for this one. We believe you have the power. You have told us to call the deacons, to anoint with oil, and ask for healing. In your name we ask you, heal Jeremy if it be your will."

Tim shared then. He quietly explained how Jeremy had been our delight, the pride of our hearts, and then how he had begun slowly to regress. He told of the many doctors and specialists who were mystified by Jeremy's case. They all knew something was wrong. But no one knew why. . . .

Tim's voice shook. He put his face in his hands and silently sobbed. I was glad I had sat next to him so I could hold his hand now. We shared our pain.

Electric is what they call the air when realness is sensed, when masks are laid down and one becomes broken before God. *Why is it we so seldom become vulnerable to one another? Does it happen only out of dreadful pain?* I wondered.

God was with us that afternoon. There. In the midst of our broken spirits. Our desire was not for Jeremy's healing at all expense. Our prayer was for God's will. Whatever it was. We laid ourselves at His feet that day asking from Him kindness, care, and strength. Indeed, when we had invited those whom we loved to the service we had said, "If God should choose to heal Jeremy it would be marvelous. If He doesn't; we need an even greater healing, the healing of our spirits to go on."

Pastor Hart anointed Jeremy's head with oil and invited all in the circle to touch him as we prayed. Jeremy squirmed. It is a difficult thing for an autistic-like child to be touched by so many.

Charity stood close to me as I held Jeremy in my lap. She put her tiny hands on Jeremy, her buddy, and squeezed her eyes shut as we all prayed for God's intervention.

Many prayed . . . brokenly, freely, all begging God for his healing power. Surely more than a grain of mustard seed of faith was expended that day.

Grandpa prayed, one of the few times I had ever heard my

father pray in public. I was deeply moved that he would pray in front of persons who were mostly strangers to him. He wept. He was bearing his own pain in seeing his first grandchild as Jeremy was.

I listened to Tim pray, then thinking of that sorrow we carry, that sorrow we never really lay down, I thought how it has made us real. We have shed our masks. The picture C.S. Lewis painted in, *The Great Divorce* seemed aptly realistic for us. I could identify with the man from hell he described who after having a chance to go to heaven chose to return to hell because the grass was so real in heaven it was excruciatingly painful to walk on.

Our reality seemed excruciatingly painful.

As I began to pray, I realized Jeremy, who never naps, had fallen asleep in my lap. I thanked God for His faithfulness. I asked God for healing of Jeremy's body as well as our spirits and that God's will would be done. I sensed a blanket of love and comfort. I felt God's presence even in the simple act of Jeremy's sleeping peacefully on my knees. He was with us. It was enough.

8

"Jeremy's on Fire!"

Temperatures in November 1982 were unseasonably high for Minnesota, but the warm weather didn't melt the cold gloom hanging over me. Tim and I had just returned from yet another conference. This time with Jeremy's Communication Interaction Disorder (CID) teachers, as well as Sheila and Henry. The CID program so close to our home had seemed a wonderful placement for Jeremy. It differed from the other schools Jeremy had attended in that most of the children here were not retarded. Basically, like Jeremy, they looked "normal" and were physically agile. What they shared in common was a pervasive communication disorder handicap.

But again our hopes for Jeremy seemed to crumble. "Jeremy's just not ready for this program," Henry had said.

"I think this kind of classroom is frustrating for Jeremy." Sheila added. "If anything, it is more difficult for him to process language now than it was when he was back with us at the Autism Program."

In two weeks Jeremy was to be transferred from the CID classroom to Bakerstown. Tim and I had reluctantly acquiesced to this, even though I'd sworn Jeremy would go to Bakerstown over my dead body last May. We felt beaten down. Sheila, sensing our anxiety, had personally assisted in finding a more appropriate placement for Jeremy at Bakerstown and we trusted her. Tim and I were relieved to discover that at least Jeremy would not be in the class that Manya Thompson had so bluntly described by saying, "The potential of these children is zero." Although we were unhappy about the transfer, we were too tired to fight anymore.

Later in the week Dr. Backus, Jeremy's pediatric neurologist, called. "Penny, we need to set up more tests for Jeremy. I talked to Sheila today and she feels Jeremy is continuing to regress. Do you and Tim see it that way?"

"Yes, I guess we do. He hardly talks at all now and he is more hyper than ever."

"That is Sheila's sense of things, too, Penny, and she is almost always right about these kiddies."

"What will happen to Jeremy if he has a regressive disease?"

"Penny, we've already tested for every regressive disease that's treatable. The ones we'll test for next are the ones we worry about. They are untreatable and extremely rare." He paused and then continued slowly, "If Sheila hadn't told me she thinks Jeremy's regressing I wouldn't even do the tests. She knows these kiddies so well though; if she thinks he is regressing I listen."

"Dr. Backus, what are you saying?" I asked him. "Are you saying Jeremy would die?"

"Yes," he answered heavily. "But, we won't know 'till we do the tests. Sometimes we don't know the cause even when the autopsy reports come in."

I struggled to understand. "But wouldn't Jeremy be uncoordinated if he had a regressive disease? He seems so healthy except for his lack of communication skills."

Dr. Backus answered carefully. "Usually children presenting with a regressive disease lose functions they previously had. Motor abilities are not necessarily affected right away. Often, one sign we see is extremely crotchety behavior. It's often extremely difficult for the family to cope with."

"I don't think Jeremy is crotchety. He's fussy sometimes, but I wouldn't describe him as crotchety."

Dr. Backus seemed encouraged by that. "That's the best news I've heard about Jeremy for a long time."

I shared with Tim my conversation with Dr. Backus. We decided Jeremy couldn't have a regressive disease. He wasn't *really* crotchety. And he wasn't going to die. It just couldn't happen. Not after all we'd been through. We put the whole issue in the back of our minds although we marked our calendar for tests to begin in December.

Two weeks later, November 21, 1982, was another beautiful fall day. The bright sun squeezed through the tiny squares of the skylight in our church sanctuary. As I listened to Pastor Hart preach, I realized it was one of the few times in the past two years I hadn't cried throughout the service. Sitting without the distractions of children in church, I felt alone with God. It was there I often journaled prayers, scrawling the grief of my soul to God.

I always tried to restrain my tears until after I left the choir loft at the front of the church, but occasionally a song would touch me and my Kleenex would soon be a wet ball. I didn't want to be exposed, to feel emotionally naked. I had always been perceived as "the strong one," and even as "strong willed" by some. The past two years I had continued to be strong. Teaching at Kids' Kottage, our latchkey daycare center, caring for Charity and Jeremy, as well as being Tim's wife, I had to be. It was only at church I felt I could be alone with God, take off my illusion of strength and talk to God as Abba—Daddy Father. *Daddy-Father help us!* I prayed.

This Sunday, the sun, the balmy day so late in November, Pastor Hart's humble spirit and encouraging words, gave me courage. I felt different. More able to cope with Jeremy's continued regression. After all, he was a sweet little boy and we truly loved him just as he was. I knew it wouldn't be easy, however. Jeremy was still not improving, but it was time to move on. We had prayed and prayed. We had spent nearly two years pouring all of our emotional energy into finding a cure for Jeremy. We had grieved when no cure was found. We had explored all the treatable medical possibilities open to us.

Yes, it was time to quit mourning. God knew we'd had our share of suffering. Hadn't He promised not to give us more than we could handle. What was that verse? I looked in my *New American Standard Version* Bible, I Corinthians 10: 13, "No temptation has overtaken you but such as is common to man; and God is faithful, who will not allow you to be tempted beyond what you are able; but with the temptation will provide the way of escape also, that ye may be able to endure it" That was it. I had always heard the verse interpreted to mean nothing would happen that one couldn't handle, including no suffering. Surely God knew we had had enough.

Please God, I prayed, *keep Jeremy safe when we can't see him. Watch over him when he runs away. Lord, we're doing the very best we can to take care of our Punky. We trust You to protect Him when we can't see him.*

We'd keep looking for an answer to Jeremy's regression, but in the meantime we needed to start living a more normal life. I looked around at others of our church body who I knew were suffering. I saw Amy, a young mother who had recently been diagnosed with multiple sclerosis. Lori, sitting with her arm around her little girl, Sharla, was divorced. Lori had lost custody in a bitter fight and was able to see her child only every other weekend. I felt the absence of my good friend Debbie, hospitalized and fighting for not only her own life, but the life of the baby still within her. We could understand some of their pain. Maybe Tim and I could start reaching out to other people's needs again.

It wasn't long until we had a chance to do just that. After church our good friends Mark and Karen Baden stopped Tim. "Hey, Tim, do you have a few minutes this afternoon to help us move our fridge to our new house?"

"Sure," Tim said. "When would you like me to come over?"

I interrupted. "Why don't you all come to our house for lunch first? You can't have much food in your fridge if it's ready to move."

Karen and I prepared lunch in our daycare center kitchen. Often when we were entertaining families with young children we chose to eat and cook there. This was especially convenient since the daycare center is connected to our home. Tim ran between our kitchen and the daycare center kitchen, one-half level below, getting the things I'd need to prepare blueberry crepes. As Karen and I talked, Jeremy with lightning speed, stuck his whole hand in the crepe batter, spilling some of it. "Jeremy, Honey, that's not for you. Where is your daddy?" Turning to Karen, I said, "Let's get these crepes going and then I'll go change his diaper. Looks like he's soaked."

Tim came down just then, "Here, I'll take Jerem' with me. I have to get the caramel rolls out of the microwave anyway."

"You and Tim are so patient," Karen remarked. "I don't know how you do it!"

Wiping the batter off the counter-top, I replied, "Tim is a lot more patient than I am. But I think we both try to save our energy for the big things." I poured a spoonful of batter on the large fry pan, watching the white mixture become golden brown. "If we got angry every time Jeremy spilled something we wouldn't have energy left to sneeze."

Tim came down with the caramel rolls in hand and was chatting with Mark for a few seconds when I heard Jeremy cry. It was the frustrated cry we were growing accustomed to.

"Tim, you better go and get him."

Tim sprinted up the short flight of stairs. As he reached the door Jeremy came bursting through. "EEEHH! EEEHH! EEEEHH!"

"He's on fire! Oh God, he's on fire!" Tim screamed. "Get a blanket!"

I ran for a blanket in the adjoining room seeing from the corner of my eye the fire leaping from Jeremy's wet diaper. *Thank God He's not potty-trained!* I thought. Jeremy's pants were gone except for around his diaper. *Where are they?* I wondered vaguely. His legs looked a shiny green and red, but not burned.

Running with the blanket, I realized Tim had already put the fire out with his bare hands, incurring deep burns.

"We've got to get his legs in water!" Karen said.

"No!" Mark argued. "His skin might fall off. He's burned too bad." Mark looked at Tim questioningly, "Tim, what do you want us to do?"

"We better not if we don't know for sure," Tim said.

Tim and Mark carried Jeremy upstairs to find the cause of the fire and see if we needed to evacuate as I called the paramedics. As I listened to the rings I wondered, *How can this be happening? Maybe I'm even over-reacting** by calling for help. "Operator!" I cried, "Please help me! My little boy is burned!"

"Is your house on fire?" the operator asked.

"No, I don't think so," I replied, my voice shaking.

"What's your address?"

Forcing myself to speak steadily I gave our street and number. *God help us!*

"Please repeat that," the voice asked.

Repeating the address, I remembered to give the cross street closest to us. "Please hurry! . . . Help us Jesus! Not my baby!"

"Someone will be there soon, dear," the kind operator assured me.

I ran upstairs to join the others. Mark held Jeremy. His anguished screams ripped at me. *Oh, God! What can I do? How can this be happening? We haven't even had lunch yet!*

Karen wound her arms around me tightly as we waited for the paramedics arrival. I clung to her. "Cry," she demanded. The sobs strangling my throat burst out.

Karen gathered her Matt and Alli and our little Charity in a circle on the carpet next to Jeremy. They prayed, "Jesus help

---

*Dr. David Ahrenholz, Co-director of the Burn Center at St. Paul Ramsey Medical Center, told us while reviewing this manuscript: "Recent research indicates that cooling reduces a burn injury if carried out within two minutes of the injury, but not later. Cool water will not hurt any thermal burn, but may make chemical burns worse.

Jeremy right now! Take care of him. Help him not to be so scared!" Tears chasing down her cheeks, Karen ended her prayer, "Help us all, dear Jesus! Help us all!"

As sirens whined from the arriving police car, I ran to collect my purse and shoes. Tim met the policeman and quickly told him what had happened. Mark carried Jeremy outside wrapped in the blanket.

"Let's wet some clean towels and wrap his legs in them," the policeman said.

The ambulance rounded the corner of Cottage Place. The siren that had always put fear in my heart now brought relief. *Please help us! Do something for my son!*

The ambulance attendants wrapped Jeremy carefully in wet towels and gently placed him on the gurney. Mark said, "I'll take care of Charity. Call us as soon as you find out anything. We'll wait here till I hear from you."

Tim and I nodded through our tears and climbed into the ambulance.

"Lights and sirens!" the paramedic said. "Hang on Mom and Dad! This is going to be a rough ride. We've gotta get your little boy to the Burn Center as fast as we can."

Tim squeezed my hand. "Maybe it won't be too bad, Honey."

I looked down at my little son, his eyes reeling with fear. His cries were almost rhythmic as he panted for breath in between his screams. "EEEH! EEEH! EEEH!" I realized he had no idea what was happening to him.

I could not be comforted. *We're good parents, God! Things like this don't happen to parents who watch their children! We prayed even today you'd protect Jeremy! Jeremy can't talk! Isn't that enough, God?*

The last shred of my childhood belief that God would protect me and mine if we fully trusted Him fragmented before my eyes. Aloneness and despair filled me up. I did not feel God's presence, yet I continued to call on His name. *"God! Jesus! Help our baby!"* I searched for a way to escape the reality at my knees. My mother heart cried, *Let me die! Let me and Jeremy die in this ambulance! Let us out! Jeremy has beautiful legs! We haven't even had our lunch yet! Let us go back and do it over again! We'll eat lunch and think about it calmly. Dear God! Give us another chance! We won't let it happen if we can just go back and do it over again!*

My thoughts fought wildly with one another as I struggled to make sense of the inconceivable events of the past ten minutes.

"Penny, we have to stay with him," Tim said, "He's so scared.

When we get to the hospital I'll go with him. If they give us
trouble, call Sheila. She'll help us if we need it." Tim was referring to what we'd already learned from the testing we'd been
through. Many medical people aren't familiar with autism and
will assume a normal looking autistic child is being uncoopera-
tive rather than realizing they really don't understand. Sheila had
given us her home phone as well as the clinic number and said,
"If you ever need a professional on your side when dealing with
medical personnel, call me."

The ambulance shrieked to a stop inside the emergency room
doors at St. Paul Ramsey Medical Center. Doctors came running
to meet us, took a quick look under the blanket and said, "Let's
get him to the Burn Center, stat!"

Tim said, "Jeremy's autistic. He can't talk. I'm going with
him!"

Tim stood near Jeremy in the elevator, saying, "It's O.K.,
Punky Boy, Daddy's here." At the double doors of the sterile unit
a nurse had stepped in front of Tim and said, "You cannot go in
there."

Tim countered, "Jeremy's autistic. He needs me! He can't
talk."

"You can't go in," she repeated resolutely, "We have to debride
(remove) his burned skin. Go and wait in the family room and
we'll come and get you when you can see him."

I stayed behind to fill out forms and to answer for the first of
hundreds of times how it happened. Through my sobbing I explained, "Jeremy is autistic-like. He climbs on things to get what
he wants because he can't talk. Today when we had company he
climbed on the stove and accidentally knocked on an element
switch. He was probably reaching for candy he thought was above
the microwave. It's directly above the stove." I stopped to blow
my nose. "I don't know how it could've happened so quickly. He
was upstairs less than two minutes."

"Was the stove gas?" the doctor asked.

"No, electric."

"It's usually a gas stove that ignites clothing." Then he told me
something we would continue to hear many times in the next two
months. "Fabrics vary greatly in their flammability. Some actually are so combustible they literally explode and then melt. This
sounds like it may be one of those cases."

The young doctor led me to the Burn Center family room. It
was a tiny box-like space lined on all four walls by orange chairs
and couches. An attractive woman of about twenty-five was sit-

ting using the phone that rested on a corner table. Nearby sat a kind looking, middle-aged woman.

Tim was waiting for me. "Did they get all the information they needed?"

"I guess so." Wouldn't they let you go in?"

"No. I tried, Penny. The nurse said they never let anyone go in. I just hope he's okay. They said they'd come and get us as soon as they're done debriding him, whatever that is."

The young woman who had been using the phone looked at us sympathetically. "They have to take the burned skin off so he won't get infection. Oh, I'm Darla. My husband, Steve, has been in here for six weeks. Try not to worry. The staff's great."

The older woman added, "They'll come and get you when they're finished. What happened? Was that your little boy they just brought down the hall?"

"Yes," Tim nodded.

"The cute little blonde? Golly, that's too bad. I just hate to see the little ones come in," said the middle-aged woman who identified herself as Madge, a farmer's wife from North Dakota.

I called my sister, Jackie.

"This is Penny." My voice broke.

"What's happened now?" she demanded.

"Oh, Jack, Jeremy got burned!"

"Oh no! Is it bad?"

"I think so. We're at the Burn Center at Ramsey." Through my tears, I told her what little I knew.

"I'm scheduled to work at the hospital tonight, Penny. I don't know if I can come down right away."

"That's okay. Would you call Mom and Dad for me?"

"Sure, and I'll try to get someone to work for me. Call back as soon as you've talked to the doctors."

I quickly dialed our friend Marie and asked her to call the leader of the prayer group and our pastors at church.

A young man wearing small preppy glasses came in and sat down as I hung up the phone. I remembered seeing him downstairs when we'd come into the emergency room.

"Hello. I'm Dr. Kernstine," he said with a Bostonian accent. "Jeremy's doing okay. We're debriding the burned tissue from his legs right now. You'll be able to see him in a few minutes."

"Doctor, how do his legs look?" Tim asked.

"Like they're badly burned."

"But he was out of our sight for only a minute—two at the most! " I interjected.

"It doesn't take long to be burned," he said sadly.

My throat tightened. "Is he going to be okay?"

"The first forty-eight hours are critical. We think he'll make it."

I drew a breath. Critical! This was serious!

The doctor interrupted my thoughts. "Do you have the brand name of the pants he was wearing? It would be helpful if we knew what the fiber content was."

"We don't. But we'll find out today," Tim said. He seemed relieved to have something concrete to do. "We have a pair exactly like them and a jacket to match at home. Thank God he wasn't wearing that. His sweater was only scorched."

"It probably was flame retardant," the doctor said. "Too bad his pants weren't."

Tim asked, "How long do you think he'll have to be in here, Doctor?"

"It's difficult to say. If everything goes well, maybe a month. If he gets an infection, that's another story."

A pretty blonde nurse poked her head in the door. "You're Jeremy's parents? You can see him now. Would you come with me?"

We walked down a long hall. One side had doors opening into what looked like small examining rooms. The other was covered with huge blown-up pictures. Red angry skin covered by clear face masks stared at me. Bloody, open flesh gaped around a skinny child's legs. Long metal pins held a young woman's shaven head immobile in a frame.

The strong smell of the Burn Center filled my nostrils. I felt as if I was going to be sick. Is this what our son's legs would look like? How could it be that only two hours ago we were in worship? *Dear God! It's Sunday afternoon. What are we doing in a place like this?*

9

"It's Not Your Fault"

The nurse led us through double swinging orange doors marked ISOLATION. As we stepped inside the smell of bleach and another distinct odor filled the air. The blonde nurse who had come to get us identified herself as Claudia. She explained how we should prepare every time we entered the Burn Center. First, we washed our hands using a foot pedal to operate the water flow. Next we put on a long yellow, cloth gown. Then, we donned a paper surgical hat and finally surgical gloves. Our personal belongings were to be bagged and tied. If we needed to leave for any reason, including going to the rest room, the process was reversed. Each time we re-entered we were to follow the same procedure.

As Claudia helped us gown I looked around the circular center. Surrounding the circular nurses station were about seven large rooms. Directly opposite the doors we entered was a short hallway opening into a solarium where a T.V. and several lounge chairs were located.

Claudia led us to a smaller room to the right of the nurses circle. "Jeremy's in here. We've given him morphine for the pain. He's kind of out of it right now," she added softly.

But as we entered, we could hear Jeremy crying in his sleep, "Eeeeh! Eeeeh!" I leaned over his bed gingerly, trying not to touch his legs carefully covered by a crisp white sheet. I sobbed, "Jesus! Oh God! Jesus! Help us!"

Tim's hands began hurting. They were black where the fabric from Jeremy's melting pants had bitten into his flesh. A young resident came in and asked a nurse to clean the wounds and bandage them there in the Burn Center. I sighed in relief. I couldn't bear the thought of Tim leaving me to go to Emergency for treatment.

Tim winced as the nurse cut the burned flesh from his hands. I watched, horrified, realizing how many times worse Jeremy's pain must have been. My soul ached for my son. I envied Tim the physical pain he could feel. I was numb. I felt as if a black hole were swallowing me up—a hole of despair.

The nurse lifted the sheet from Jeremy's legs. Even with the thick bandages covering them they looked like the legs of a scrawny, malnourished child. I could see that big gouges of flesh had been removed beside his knee and calf of his right leg. *Dear God! He has beautiful legs!* "Why do his legs look like that?" I gasped.

"The burned flesh had to be removed to prevent the dead tissue from rotting and causing infection," she replied. "Initially, we worry most about loss of body fluids through the burned areas." She pointed to Jeremy's bandages already filling with oozing liquid and blood. "That's why he's getting liquids through an I.V. See, right over here."

I nodded to show her I understood. As she left, Jeremy cried out again, tossing his blonde head, "Eeehh!"

I cringed. *How did this happen?* Again and again my mind struggled to comprehend. My thoughts seemed scrambled. I wondered, "Is this what it's like to go crazy? Could this be my escape from . . ." My mind refused to form the picture of what had happened in our kitchen only an hour before. In my mental jumble, I groped for strength to face what had happened. *Oh, God, how can I escape? Punky's in pain! Dear God! Help me! I can't leave him here alone. He needs me! Hold me God!* In those moments of crying out to God, sobbing softly over my son's still form, I didn't care who heard me. I had to make a choice. . . . In the end, it wasn't a choice for sanity, but a choice against insanity.

The same nurse appeared at the door. "I need to change his bandages again. You probably will want to leave."

As we prepared to go, Dr. Kernstine, who had spoken to us earlier in the family room, said, "Do you have a minute? I'd like to talk to you about what will be happening with Jeremy in the next few days."

We sat down with him and another male doctor on the barstools in front of the circular nurses' station. I felt relieved to see the nurse shut the door to Jeremy's room before changing his bandages. I wasn't ready to see his legs. I just couldn't face that yet.

"Jeremy will probably have major surgery on Tuesday to debride all of the damaged tissue," Dr. Kernstine said. "We usually wait a day or two following a burn of this size. Besides, Monday is clinic day so we usually don't do surgery that day."

I thought, *I could care less when clinic day is. This is my son.*

Dr. Kernstine continued, "We may be able to graft the same day if his legs look good and healthy when we get in there. First, we'll get through the next forty-eight hours. Then we'll worry about getting those legs cleaned up so his grafts will take."

Tim asked, "Doctor, how much pain is he in?"

"We do everything we can to minimize the pain. Jeremy is getting morphine now which will help, but I won't kid you. It is painful."

Tim's face contorted. Tears filled his eyes.

"Jeremy was burned pretty deeply. Nearly to the muscle," Dr. Kernstine said sympathetically. "Most of his nerve endings are gone. At this point, he may be feeling less pain than you think."

"Eeeeeh!" We could hear Jeremy moaning in spite of the morphine, as the nurse changed his bandages.

I wondered: *Why is he crying if it doesn't hurt that bad? Why did the nurse say they'll give him as much morphine as they dare to?* But aloud I only asked, "Dr. Kernstine, how much of Jeremy's legs are burned?"

He replied, "Both legs are burned from his feet to near his genitals with the exception of the outer thigh of the left leg which is only superficially burned. The burns on and around both knees on both legs are very deep. They will be difficult to heal. The other area I worry about is the heel cord of the left leg. It's completely exposed and will probably give us the most trouble."

"What do you mean?" Tim asked.

"Well, that cord has little tissue around it. It's the tendon that needs to stretch to walk properly. Let's not worry about that now. You've got enough to deal with for today. Getting back to your earlier question." He hesitated slightly. "I would guess about 16-20% of Jeremy's body is burned."

Tim hesitated. "He isn't in any danger? I mean it isn't life-threatening is it?"

The doctor answered in a professional tone, "The next forty-eight hours are critical for kidney or respiratory failure. It's quite a shock to the system to be burned this badly. This is a good unit, however, and we will watch him very closely." Pausing briefly he pushed the preppy glasses higher on his nose. "I think he'll make out fine . . . as long as he doesn't get infection."

There was that word again, "infection." It was to become the word that would haunt us for the next weeks and months as our life revolved around 5 East—The Burn Center at St. Paul Ramsey Medical Center.

My eyes filled with tears that ran into my lap. My nose was running, and my Kleenex were gone. The young doctor handed me a tissue. "You blame yourself don't you?" he asked.

I nodded. "If only I had been watching him those few seconds. Dear God! He was out of our sight only a minute."

He put his arm firmly around my shoulders and gently shook me. "Mrs. Giesbrecht, it was not your fault."

"But, if I'd only kept him with me. We wouldn't even be here," I argued.

"Look, I know what you're going through," he said quietly.

I thought of the testing, the hopes we'd had for Jeremy smashed at our feet . . . . Now, this! How could he know what I was going through? I felt old. Old, and tired, and terrified.

The young doctor interrupted my thoughts as he repeated, "I know what you're going through, but it's not your fault." He faltered. "I know, because my brother is like this." He gestured to the room where Jeremy lay mercifully drugged with morphine. "My mother has suffered so much guilt without cause. You're doing the same thing." He spat the words out. "I want you to say to me, 'It's not my fault'."

I was moved by the compassion of the young doctor. By his own sharing of his pain. Haltingly I repeated, "It's . . . not . . . my . . . fault."

"Say it again!" he demanded, still holding my shoulders firmly.

"It's . . . n . . . n . . . not . . . m . . . m . . . my . . . fault."

My stiff shoulders relaxed. I sobbed softly looking into his eyes. In them, I saw not judgment, but compassion. It was the beginning of release from the cumbersome guilt I carried. Tim sat beside me carrying his own guilt, but as was his character kept it to himself and dealt with it alone. Although still feeling queasy, I went back to Jeremy's room for another check on "Punky" before leaving the Center.

Jackie, my sister, had been excused from her work as an R.N. at another hospital, and was gowning to come into the Center. She came and stood beside me. "Poor baby," she murmured as she looked down at her nephew.

"I need to get out of here, Jack."

"I'll stay with him for awhile," she said.

I left, knowing he was in good hands with his daddy and his

auntie who was not only a nurse but had even worked in the Burn Center on occasion.

I was glad someone else was there to comfort Tim. I was concerned for him knowing how he must hurt for his only son, but I was so overwhelmed with my own grief, I didn't have anything left to give Tim. I thought of the counseling we'd had in dealing with Jeremy's autism. We'd been encouraged not to depend upon support from each other. It helped us both to not feel resentful when we realized our expectations of each other might be unrealistic at times. I was grateful Jackie was here for both of us to lean on now.

In the family room, Madge, the farmer's wife from North Dakota, whom I had met earlier, told me about how her husband was burned.

"Al was working on a combine when the carburetor suddenly exploded. My son saw the fire, grabbed Al and rolled in the dirt with him. Sometimes I think, what if my son hadn't been there? He saved Al's life."

Madge still had a girlishness about her. Maybe it was her slightly upturned pug nose, or the soft drawl of her low voice as she spoke. As we talked I learned she had seven children, one of whom was born severely handicapped. She spoke lovingly of this daughter, Bernadette. Proudly she produced her picture. Although five years old in the photo, she looked the size of an infant and weighed just fourteen pounds.

"From the time she was born we were told Bernadette would die. They didn't expect her to live a year. I never left her but once. Al begged me to get away. I left for the weekend on a women's retreat from our church. She died . . . that Sunday."

I felt sad. I wanted to convey that I cared, but I didn't know how. I was so tired. All I could really think of was my son lying in the Burn Center. Finally I simply said, "That must have been so hard for you."

Madge nodded. "It was. I always said I didn't want to be there when she died. Maybe God knew when she should go. But, still I wonder sometimes. . . . If I'd been there, would she have died?"

I knew what she meant. I still wondered. If I'd been upstairs with Jeremy, would he have been burned. If I loved God more, would He have protected him? I knew what she meant. Pangs of guilt kept coming back.

Madge showed me a stack of family pictures. I wanted to show her I cared and tried to concentrate politely, but I felt drained of emotion. I couldn't remember a time in my life when I had nothing inside to draw from to give. It scared me.

Another woman entered the room and introduced herself as Darla, whose husband Steve was in the Center. Being Sunday, both Darla and Madge had many relatives from out of town, visiting their husbands. Only two could visit at a time in the Burn Center, so much of Darla and Madge's time on Sundays was spent in the family room.

I asked Darla, "How did your husband get burned?" She seemed so happy-go-lucky. So vibrant. I thought, *Steve must not be burned as badly as Al.*

Darla talked faster than anyone I'd ever heard before. Her hands raced with her voice visually describing her words. "He was burned in a pipe. Steve is, I mean was, a pipe-fitter." She smiled as she corrected herself. "He was working on the big gasification plant they're building in North Dakota. He was so skinny. He's even skinnier now, " she laughed. "Anyway, he got picked to go inside this pipe so he could weld it from the inside. The guys put oxygen in for him to breathe and that started the fire. It took them thirty minutes to get him out so he got burned pretty bad."

"That's awful." I gasped. "Is he . . . will he . . . be okay?"

"I almost lost Steve a couple of times, but they pulled him through every time. He's doing a lot better now. Isn't he, Madge?"

Naively, I asked, "Will he go home soon?"

"Oh, it's too early to say. Steve will need lots more surgery. Especially to rebuild his face."

I thought of the pictures in the hall.

Darla whistled softly. "His eyelids and nose and one ear were burned off and his right arm was burned so bad they couldn't save it. But, my hubby's alive and that's all I care about now."

"You seem like you're doing so well. I mean—" I faltered searching for the right words.

"Oh kid. You'll get tough, too," Darla answered quickly, "You should have seen ME the night they flew Steven in.

"Dr. Ahrenholz sat right where you are, and told me, 'I'm sorry, but I don't think your husband's going to make it. He's just burned too badly.'

"I told him. 'Look, he's only twenty-five. He's got a two-year-old son. He is NOT going to die! You don't know us! We're buddies, and we don't give up without a fight. You have to pull him through.' "

Darla paused remembering. She lowered her voice. "Dr. Ahrenholz started to cry. Can you believe that? Geezus! This doctor doesn't know me from Adam and he starts to cry. He said, 'I'll do everything I can. I promise you.' " She looked me squarely in the eyes. "Now, your little sweetheart wasn't burned as bad as Steve. He's going to be just fine. They pulled my hubby through and they'll pull your baby through too."

Darla seemed so incredibly together. Here she was just a young woman dealing with all this and yet still seemed so vibrant and full of life. She gave me hope that someday, I too, would no longer feel dead.

Later, I was sitting alone in the family room while Tim and Jackie took their turn staying with Jeremy in the Center. Madge's sister from Kettle River came in and sat down.

"That your little boy that just came in today?" she boomed.

"Yes, it is," I said, secretly hoping I wouldn't have to tell the story again. She didn't look at all like Madge. Madge's tiny frame sharply contrasted with the much larger structure of her sister. Although each had a deep voice and a distinct accent, Madge's was soft, a contrast to the vociferous speech of her sister.

"Madge told me all about your little boy." She clucked her tongue. "It's just terrible. Such a cute little boy. Just a doll, he is."

"Thank you," I mumbled. "Jeremy always had such beautiful legs. I always said, he should be a girl."

"It's just not fair," she declared. "Such a good little boy to have to go through all this."

I liked this big, strong woman. I liked her sincerity. She didn't even know Jeremy, yet she had guessed that he was a sweet, innocent child. I liked her sound judgment.

She continued. "I've got two kids downstairs in the lobby. Twins." She raised her eyebrows shaking her head resolutely. "Meanest kids you ever saw."

"How old are they?" I asked.

"They're ten now, but they've been mean a long time," she thundered. "Practically since they was babies."

I smiled, thinking she was kidding me, but she assured me she wasn't. As she shared some of their escapades I began to understand.

Her voice resonated in the small room. "Yup, I told them twins, 'There's cops here. Lot's of 'em! They're gonna be watchin' you to see if you make trouble.' She smiled cunningly now, "I think they're real scared. Last time I checked on 'em they weren't up to one thing," she said shaking her head in amazement.

Not knowing how to respond I asked, "Do you have just two children?"

She seemed shocked. "Two? Heck no! I've got six older ones at home. That's how the twins got so mean. All six o' the big ones taught them twins every mean thing they ever knew."

In spite of the pain in my heart, I laughed. I couldn't believe it. I laughed!

Jackie and Tim came together from the Center then and told me of their plan to get our car and bring it to the hospital. Tim put his arms around me and hugged me tightly. I could feel the tightness of his muscles. "How you doin'?" I asked.

"I'm okay," he responded.

Even now Tim was the strong one, sitting with Jeremy for hours without relief. Even though Tim's reserved nature held his feelings in check, I knew that his pain for our son ran as deeply as my own.

Many details remained to be cared for. After Tim came into the family room, we decided not to open our daycare center the following day. It had never been closed before, but we needed that one day to make decisions. We began calling the parents of the children. Most were more than business acquaintances. They were friends.

Tim seemed incredibly calm as he talked to each parent on his list. Calmly he repeated Jeremy's story over and over. And each time I told what had happened it seemed a little easier. The inevitable shock of the voice on the other end of the telephone line, however, at times would cause my voice to break and I would cry again.

Between our calls, my parents got through to us.

"Do you want Dad to come down now?" Mom said. "I've got pneumonia. The doctor said I have to stay in bed and rest at least a couple of weeks. It's tearing me up inside that I can't come right down."

My mother never got sick. *Why now?* I thought, but I answered numbly. "It's okay. Dad had better stay there with you." I knew how much Dad hated driving alone in the city.

Mom reminded me that the prayer groups in their area churches had all been activated.

"They say the next forty-eight hours are critical and after that we need to pray he won't get infection," I told her. "Tell them to pray that his grafts will take."

After calling Tim's parents in Canada and his brother, a missionary with Wycliffe Bible Translators in Australia, we knew people literally all over the world were praying for Jeremy. All were instructed, "Pray that his grafts will take." Surely with thousands praying for him. Surely God would at least grant us this one request.

As we finished our calls a nurse came in and said, "It's almost time for the cafeteria to close. Have you two eaten yet today?"

I looked at my watch. It was five to six. Tim answered for both of us. "I guess we haven't. We didn't ever eat lunch and we didn't eat breakfast before church. Maybe we should try and eat."

In the elevator, Tim pulled me close to him. He whispered in my ear, "It's so hard to believe. It happened so fast."

The food in the cafeteria looked good, though expensive. I was glad I had the checkbook. The smell of fried chicken and gravy suddenly made me feel hungry. We loaded our trays with salad, golden chicken, and white mashed potatoes.

The man at the cash register said, "Hurry up, we're ready to close." *Doesn't he know my son is burned?* I thought.

Tim took the checkbook and said, "Who should I make this out to?"

"We don't take checks," the man replied brusquely. "If you don't have cash, you don't eat."

Tim looked embarrassed. I said, "Look, we came in here by ambulance. Our son was burned. We didn't have time to get cash. We didn't even know we'd be here." I looked at him in desperation.

"Doesn't matter." His eyes were filled with disgust. "No cash. No food."

Humiliated, we left our filled trays and walked out of the cafeteria.

remy at 2½ with
1arity. We weren't
.duly alarmed that he
it saying new words.
e thought it was just a
age."

Two beautiful kids--Jeremy, 4
and Charity, 2--who love each
other. Canadian Rockies in the
background.

my--home from
Burn Center for
stmas.

Father and son at "the farm."

Goin' for a cruise.

Mother and son at "the farm."

remy swinging with his
sters in our backyard.

If only we knew what
he's thinking.

family in February, 1988: Me, Jeremy, Tim, Charity, and Angele.

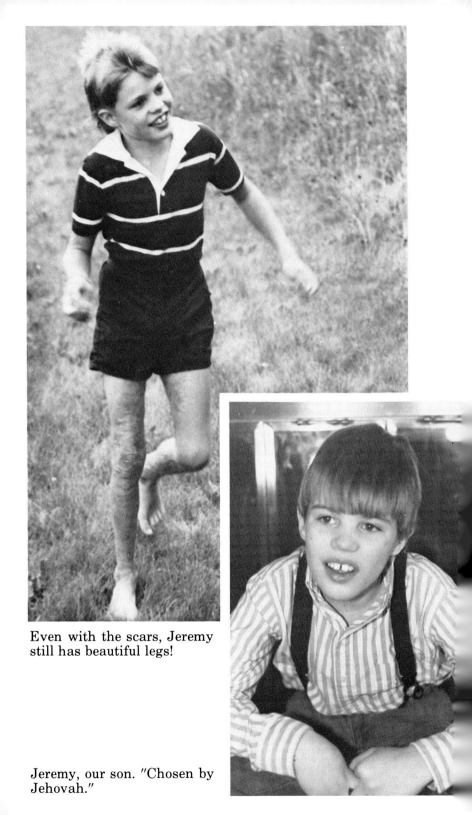

Even with the scars, Jeremy
still has beautiful legs!

Jeremy, our son. "Chosen by
Jehovah."

10

The Bond of Suffering

We returned from the cafeteria, heads hanging low. Mike Bortel, our associate pastor and Sunday school teacher, was waiting for us. "Hi, you two. How is he doing? I just got here. I wanted to see if there's anything I can do for you?"

We sat down together in the family room. We trusted Mike and knew that his life experience helped him to understand what we were going through.

"Mike, how could this happen? We prayed God would protect Jeremy. I prayed that this morning in church in fact." I began to cry softly again.

"I don't know, Penny. There is no answer to why." He sighed. "The longer I'm in the ministry the fewer easy answers I have."

"Do you believe God had a purpose in letting Jeremy get burned today?" I asked.

Mike was thoughtful as he answered. "No, I don't think God wanted Jeremy to get burned, anymore than I think God wanted my mom to be so ill and so lonely that she would commit suicide. Being a Christian doesn't make us immune to the laws of nature, brokenness, or the disease and poverty of the world. There just aren't any guarantees that tragedy won't touch our lives. I would like to believe there are, but it just doesn't match with life."

"I guess I agree with that, Mike," Tim said, "but how does the verse that says, 'all things work together for good to them that love God,' fit in with the reality of tragedy?"

"Yeah," I interjected. "How could there be any good great enough to explain what Jeremy is going through in there? My God! I can't even stand to hear him cry. His legs look like deformed sticks." I blew my nose noisily. "I don't think God did this to Jeremy. I think maybe what we've been hearing about God causing suffering for this reason or that reason is a farce. As far as I'm concerned if God does 'purpose' things like this, that kind of god can go to Hell!"

Tim whistled softly. "You know Penny, Mike. She doesn't beat around the bush, does she?"

Mike didn't appear surprised by my strong words. He only said, "I think the way that verse has been commonly interpreted misrepresents it's true meaning. I know I'm a better counselor because of what happened to my mom. But, I'd much rather have my mom here, than be the best counselor. You and Tim too, will be better able to help other people because of what you've gone through. You already have helped people in the Beta class because of Jeremy's regression."

I interrupted, "But, that doesn't make it 'good' that your mom committed suicide or that Jeremy was burned, does it Mike? I mean, just because God can bring good out of something bad— doesn't make the bad good."

"That's right. So the truth of Romans 8:28, the verse you quoted earlier, Tim, when applied to real life situations, affirms that God can work through the bad as well as the good. That is far different than glibly saying, 'all things work together for good,' therefore all that happens is good."

Mike put an arm around Tim and me as he said, "We'll be praying for you at church. Is there anything else I can do for you tonight?"

"No. Thanks for coming, though. It really means a lot to us. We know you care," Tim said.

"Yeah, Mike, thanks for coming. Thanks for listening."

Karen and Marie arrived a few minutes later bringing Charity and a basket of sandwiches and fruit. How glad we were to see them.

We hugged Charity tightly. "Where's Jeremy?" she demanded. "Jeremy wants to come home?"

Though she was only two, we explained to her in some detail what she could expect to happen in the following days.

"Jeremy wants to sleep in his own bed," she asserted.

Jackie had offered to keep Charity for at least the week. Although I knew she was in good hands I reluctantly said goodbye as she left with Tim and Jackie to pack her suitcase. Tim would bring back our car so we would have a vehicle to get home from the hospital later that evening. Although we had wanted to stay with Jeremy, we were told that under no condition were parents permitted to stay with their children in the Burn Center. This was clearly to minimize the risk of infection to the patients.

I ate a sandwich from Marie's basket only because I knew I should eat. The hunger that had seized me in the cafeteria had gone as soon as I took a bite, but I continued to chew under the scrutiny of my two dear friends. I noticed their eyes were red and swollen. Vaguely I thought, I probably don't look so great myself.

"Penny, I feel so awful," Karen said. "Maybe it wouldn't have happened if you hadn't been hurrying to feed us."

"That's nonsense," I said. "It just happened. I can't believe it happened. But it did. And it's nobody's fault."

I felt tired. My head pounded. I tried to focus on the conversation, but my mind skipped around.

I told them the story of Madge's twins, finishing with, " 'Of course I got more kids. How do you think they got so mean? The big ones taught them twins every mean thing they knew.' " The three of us laughed and cried. . . . We needed to do both.

After Tim returned with the car, Karen and Marie left. Then Pastor Hart arrived. He shared with us the concern of our friends in the church service that evening and listened quietly as we explained the events of the day. Then he prayed and slipped away. We felt thankful for such wonderful pastors. All of the sermons in the world could never mean more than their being with us today.

It was time for us to leave. We gowned in the Center and went in to kiss our little Punky Boy one more time. Lovingly Tim stroked Jeremy's blonde hair. I pulled at his arm. "Tim, we need to go."

I, too, found it difficult to go home. As our car took us closer and closer to "where it happened," panic filled me. Tim reminded me that Mark had cleaned up since the accident. I wanted the couch and carpeting that were burned in the fire taken out. I was afraid to see them again. Yet I knew this wasn't practical and was somewhat comforted by the fact that Tim had already been home to pack Charity's things.

It was nearly midnight when we pulled into the driveway. I had to force myself to go in. Grimly we examined the burned spots in the carpet and the couch. We pieced together the route Jeremy had taken once he saw fire, following the trail the burning pieces of his pants had made as they fell.

When I saw the stack of towels and blankets we'd wrapped around Jeremy's burned legs, I felt nauseous. What if his skin was in the blankets? I didn't look. I crumpled them and threw them in the washer. I washed them twice. I folded clothes. It was so quiet in the house . There was nothing to do. *We should be checking on Jeremy.* Then I'd remember where he was. Each time a wave of agony would sweep through me.

Tim called the hospital. They said, "He's stable. Try to sleep."

I went to bed, but I couldn't sleep. As soon as I shut my eyes I'd see the fire around Jeremy and hear Tim screaming, "He's on fire! God, he's on fire!" My heart cried out, *God, I can't handle this! I can't stand it. I'm so afraid.*

I remembered hearing in a psychology class in college that often a therapist would lead a patient through something they were afraid to remember until eventually it held no power over them.

I struggled to recall the events of the day, but each time I'd get to the fire, my mind would stop. *No, it's too painful!* After dozens of tries I was able to see Tim at the bottom of the stairs, his face filled with terror, screaming, "He's on fire!" I saw Jeremy standing at the door, his pants in flames at his diaper.

"EEEHH!" he cried gasping for breath in between his frantic screams.

I felt the heaviness of my legs as I struggled to run to get a blanket.

I heard myself calling for an ambulance and screaming out to God to help us.

I saw again Karen and the kids praying in a circle on the floor. I forced my mind to look at Jeremy's shiny green and red legs. I willed myself to recall the terror in his eyes—the ambulance ride—the hospital.

Again and again I recalled the accident until my face flopped on the pillow exhausted. I had faced what had happened. I had retraced it all and survived.

The next morning we arose early and drove straight to the Burn Center. Tim dropped me off at the big glass doors and went back to park the car. I hurried up to 5 East, carefully avoiding the pictures in the hall as I passed.

Jeremy was in the solarium with bright sunlight engulfing him. He was sitting up. With his legs covered by a white blanket, I could almost forget he'd been burned. A tube in his nose and an I.V. pole did little to quell the relief I felt as I saw my son looking so well.

An older man with a thick shock of white hair sat near him. Heavy blankets covered his legs as well. His hands and arms had thick white bandages around them. "Hi, I'm Al," he said. "Jeremy and I are just watching Sesame Street together." I realized he was Madge's husband.

Tim joined us. A nurse came and said, "You must be Jeremy's parents. Would you like to hold him?"

Tim responded quickly, "Sure, can you help me get him on my lap?" I was glad Tim had volunteered. I felt afraid to hold my son. Afraid I might hurt him.

"He looks so aware. Look, Penny! He's not avoiding looking at me."

Seeing Tim hold Jeremy gave me courage. I took my turn to cradle him, tubes carefully laid to Jeremy's side. A young woman walked into the solarium just then. A hard plastic mask enclosed her face. A metal band encircling her bald head connected to a rod bracing her neck. Ace-bandages covered every visible part of her body.

"Hi," I said, trying not to stare at the cigarette she held in her bandaged hands. *Dear God! How can anyone smoke after being burned like that?*

Without acknowledging my greeting, she looked at us with hollow, unseeing eyes. Abruptly, she stood up and stalked out of the room.

"Ann doesn't talk," Al noted. "She was burned in a cabin and her young son died in the explosion. She seems a little nervous." He paused smiling kindly. "We try to include her, but she never talks to anyone . . . except the nurses, if she wants something."

"Why the steel rod on the back of her neck?" I asked. It looks so uncomfortable."

"They say it's to keep the scar tissue from pulling her head down toward her shoulders."

Al told us about others in the Center. Some were in isolation because they had a germ no one else had. Isolation from the other patients prevented infection from spreading.

"Being in isolation must be awfully lonely," Al sympathized. "It's so much easier when we can help each other through this experience."

Some in the Center had been burned in explosions with machinery, Al told us. One woman had set herself on fire while standing in a garbage can. She died at the Burn Center. A small child had been burned with hot grease. We sat incredulous as we heard the stories.

It was frightening to realize the potential danger for explosion. We heard many people are burned from explosions caused by putting gas in a hot lawn mower.

I thought, *How many times have I done that?* "One young boy dropped a tool in a garage that had gas fumes in it. The spark ignited the fumes and exploded. The boy was seriously injured. Many children had been burned by their clothes, as was Jeremy. I glanced down at him. He was drowsy. A nurse walked in and remarked, "He's pretty drugged up. We'll give him as much morphine as possible these next few days." Carefully, she fluffed the pillows elevating his legs.

Curious about the information Al had just shared, I asked the nurse, "Aren't there federal laws governing flame-retardant fabrics?" She told us the federal rules are so lax that newspaper passes the safety standards. I shuddered. Newspaper burns so fast.

While we talked, Ann walked back in, plopped down, got up, marched off, and then came back to repeat the routine, all while puffing on a cigarette through her plastic mask.

The third morning after Jeremy's accident we entered the Center with our arms loaded with books and toys from home.

"Looks like you've got your arms full," Claudia, the perky, blonde nurse, exclaimed. "Here, let me get those for you while you get gowned up."

She pointed to a room across the circle. "By the way, Jeremy's in that room now."

"What?" I thought. *Why, that's Ann's room.* I walked inside and leaned down to kiss Jeremy's pale face. Ann was pacing back and forth from the room to the nurse's station stopping occasionally to speak savagely to a nurse.

"So she can talk," I said to Tim.

I waited for Ann to go to the solarium before cornering Claudia, "Why was Jeremy moved?" I asked.

"We have to have other rooms empty in case of an emergency."

How could they put my little boy so badly burned in a room with that chain-smoking woman?

I spent the rest of the afternoon trying to make conversation with Jeremy's new roommate. Occasionally, she would grace me with a terse one-word answer. Tim convinced me that we should wait and see how it would go rather than demand a non-smoking roommate for our son. "After all," he said, "she doesn't seem too thrilled with the idea of having Jeremy in her room either."

Dozens of cards decorated her walls. "You have so many beautiful cards, Ann. You must have a lot of friends who care about you." Ann looked at me. For the first time she really looked at me. A short time later she set her tape player on Jeremy's bedside table.

"Here, he can listen to tapes on my recorder. My father just gave it to me this weekend."

I was touched.

The phone rang many times that afternoon. Late in the·day a friend from church called. "Penny, when I heard I was dumbfounded!"

In spite of the severity of the situation, I smiled. It would take something pretty major for Bill to be dumbfounded.

"I thought, how can this happen to poor little Jeremy? But, then God showed me that He is going to burn the neurological problems right out of Jeremy! You just have to have faith."

My hand tightened on the receiver. *Jeremy might not even live.* I looked at him as he lay in Tim's arms crying out occasionally from the blessed stupor of morphine. *Doesn't Bill realize what my son is going through? Nothing, not even Jeremy becoming normal again is worth the agony he's suffering. Are we Christians that anxious to put our lives on a shelf marked, "CASE CLOSED?" Is it so imperative to have "the answer" that lunacy can overtake people's minds?*

Numbly I said, "Thanks for thinking of us. I . . . need to go."

Tuesday night, two days after the fire, Tim pulled Jeremy around in a little red fire-engine wagon. I pushed the pole that carried the I.V. medication as well as the high energy liquid which dripped through a tube running through his nose directly into his stomach. Jeremy seemed comforted by the movement and would cry out, "Eeeeeeh!" in a weary voice when we stopped.

Each time we rounded the circle I saw Ann, puffing on her cigarette, pacing back and forth in Jeremy's room, like a tiger in a cage. When she finally passed us on her way to the solarium, I said, "Hi, Ann. How are you?"

She stared at the floor. "Okay."

Circling again and again we looked in the rooms off the circular nurses station. We were growing close to these people and their families even though we'd been in the Burn Center just a few days. There was a bond. We all knew the terrible shock, the reality that nothing would be the same again. Together we grieved over the loss of smooth, soft skin. Together we rejoiced in life. Yet, we all asked the same questions. *Why, God? Why did it happen?*

As we passed the room where the burn patients were bathed

every morning, I remembered what Marie, Jeremy's favorite nurse, had told me, "You can tell the time by feeling the tension in this unit. In the morning before the baths it's quiet. The atmosphere is strained; you know what they're thinking about. When bath time is over and everyone's finished the feeling is one of celebration. 'It's over! I made it through!' Then at supper I feel the tension again. The patients often have a hard time sleeping knowing as soon as they wake up they have to face the bath room."

I remembered having a small burn on my finger and how excruciating the pain was when soaked in water. No wonder the burn patients dreaded these baths. It wasn't only the water. The wounds had to be scrubbed clean in bath water treated with diluted bleach. If the blood tests were off, sometimes salt was added to the water to prevent chemical imbalances. I shuddered.

The room was big. Two bath tubs were installed on opposite sides of the room with a moveable curtain between them. It seemed so public, but then it was.

A photographer came routinely to keep track of the progress of the burns. Doctors and residents, nurses and orderlies were all present at the painful bath time. The Burn Center afforded no privacy.

Visitors weren't allowed in the Center in the morning unless their family member was in critical condition. Exceptions were not made. When we begged to come early because of Jeremy's autism, the answer from the staff always was, "There's nothing you can do for him at bath time. You have enough to deal with without memories of that."

My mind was busy as we rounded the circle again and again. I gazed with sympathy into the isolation room where a single special education teacher lay. A victim of cerebral palsy, she had been unable to get out of a scalding bath by herself. When help arrived, it was too late. She loved children, particularly handicapped children. Marie, Jeremy's favorite nurse, often took Jeremy in his wagon to the teacher's window so she could see him.

Rounding the corner by the solarium we nearly bumped into Ann. "It's cold in our room," she reported. "Tell the nurses to put more covers out for Jeremy."

"Thank you, Ann. We will," Tim said. She marched off, her face expressionless.

"I've gotta sit for awhile, Tim," I said, pulling Jeremy into the solarium.

"Eeeeeeeehhhhh!" he cried.

"He's not going for it, Penny. He just wants to keep moving."
So we kept on making the seemingly endless circles. It was the
one thing we could do to help Jeremy.

Ann neared us again. "Ann, how were you burned?" I asked.
We had heard she'd never talked about the fire or her little boy to
anyone in the six weeks she'd been in the Center. Large brown
eyes peered at me through the plastic mask. She opened her
mouth as if to respond and snapped it shut. Then she spun
around and stalked off to her room.

Tim shrugged. "Maybe it's too tough for her to remember,
Hon."

Moving on we saw Darla discarding her contaminated gown as
she left her husband's room. Steve was one of the patients in
isolation so only Darla and medical personnel could visit him.
Darla spent every waking minute by his side almost as if willing
him to live. He had a trach tube in his throat and couldn't talk.
Darla talked to him, however, often reading the many letters and
cards he received.

Stopping Jeremy's wagon, we said, "Hi, Darla. How's it going?"

She was crying. "Oh, I'm okay." She wiped her tears with her
sleeve. "Poor Papa. I made him so sad tonight."

"Darla, is everything okay?" Tim patted Darla's shoulder with
a gloved hand.

"I'm just tired," she said, wearily tugging at her surgical cap
causing her long black hair to tumble out. "I said, 'Papa, I'm so
sad you're so sick.' Then I just started crying. I never let Papa see
me cry before. Then ya know what my Honeybun did?"

"What?"

"He took his little stub arm and put it around my shoulder and
tapped it as if to say, 'It's okay, Mama. We'll make it.' Darla's
reddened eyes looked into ours.

"Geezuz! Now I got you cryin', too."

When Darla left, Ann walked up to us. Her face was expressionless; her voice flat. "It was a gas explosion. We were in a
cabin. My little boy, he looked like Jeremy."

"Where is your little boy, Ann?" I spoke carefully not wanting
to overstep her confidence.

"He died in the cabin. AA . . . ndy loved tractors," she said in a
quiet voice.

Tears filled my eyes. I reached out to touch her. Tim said,
"Ann, that must have been so hard for you. I can't imagine how
hard it would be to lose Jeremy."

Her big eyes stared from behind the clear plastic mask. Although her face still seemed expressionless, her eyes were glazed as tears slid from her cheeks. "He's in heaven now. He's better off there."

"Yes, Ann, We believe Andy is in heaven too. Someday you'll see him again."

As Ann walked away again we felt humbled. Discreetly we reported to a nurse what Ann had shared so her psychiatrist could be alerted.

That night as we kissed our Punky Boy goodbye and tucked him in for the night, Ann offered, "I'll cover Jeremy if he get's cold."

Marie, the nurse, told us the following morning that Ann got up several times during the night, tersely instructing the nurses to give Jeremy more blankets or to check his I.V. "Every time he cried out," Marie said, "Ann jumped up and was beside him."

We never did ask that Jeremy be moved to a new room.

On Wednesday, three days after the fire, we signed consent forms for Jeremy's surgery. We were hopeful it would be his only one.

A doctor explained, "We have taken the precaution of ordering quite a bit of blood for Jeremy. The danger in this kind of surgery is that there is a fair amount of blood loss when we remove the burned tissue. We just need to be prepared."

After Jeremy was wheeled down to surgery we stopped at the cafeteria to pick up a roll and coffee. A pretty dark-haired woman came over and put her arm around me.

"Jenny!" I smiled at our new neighbor who had just moved in across the street, "What are you doing here? I didn't recognize you in your hospital garb."

"I work here. I'm a surgical technologist. In fact, I was looking for you. I requested to be in on Jeremy's surgery."

"How did you know Jeremy was burned?" Tim queried.

"We saw the ambulance come. I could tell it looked like a burn injury from our yard. Then we talked to your friend, Mark, after you left in the ambulance and he told us all about it."

"I'm so glad you'll be there with him, Jenny," I said. "I'm feeling pretty scared."

"He's in good hands here," Jenny replied. "This is rated as one of the best burn centers in the nation."

"That's good to hear," Tim said.

"I have to go now. I've got the operating room all warmed up for Jeremy so he won't get too cold. Try not to worry."

We waited for the surgery to end. Several long hours passed.

Finally we were called up to the family room to wait for Jeremy to come out of the anesthesia.

When at last we saw him he looked at us hazily. His skin was white. His legs oozed red fluid through the bandages and sheets covering his legs.

Dr. Ahrenholz looked tired as he stepped into the room. "Jeremy did all right. We couldn't graft today, but we cleaned his legs up. In a couple of days we'll graft skin from a donor site. We'll probably use his sides and back for donor skin."

My relief that the surgery was over was mixed with disappointment that Jeremy would have to endure another surgery. It seemed nothing ever went the easy way for Punky.

Carole, Jeremy's former tutor from Bethel College, came to see Jeremy that day bringing a sign she'd made. It said: "JESUS LOVES YOU! PUNKY BOY!" We taped it above his bed. It helped us remember Jesus was suffering with Jeremy and also with us.

11

"Dear God, Where Are You?"

Thanksgiving Day dawned cool and clear. My sister, Jackie, arranged to bring Tim and me turkey dinner at home. After visiting Jeremy in the hospital in the morning we planned to meet Jackie, my nieces, and Charity there. It would be the first time we'd seen Charity in four days.

Jeremy seemed to be recovering nicely from his first surgery. We felt optimistic after hearing from doctors and nurses alike how "good" his legs looked.

As we prepared to leave the Center for home, a young nurse said, "Why don't you take Jeremy with you?"

"What?" we asked incredulously.

"Why don't you take him home for a couple of hours." Noting our shocked expressions, she added, "He won't break, you know."

"I don't know if we should. It's kind of cold out," Tim said.

"Go on, warm your car up and bring it right to the emergency doors. We'll wrap him in blankets and he'll be just fine."

It was difficult to get Jeremy placed in the car so his legs could be elevated. Elevation of the burned area lessened the pain because it forced blood volume away from that area.

Jeremy cried all the way home. He seemed so afraid that we'd hurt him. I tried desperately to support his legs so he would be comfortable, but nothing I did seemed to help. I looked at Tim helplessly. "What if we have an accident? Why did we let her talk us into this?"

"Maybe he'll do better once we get him home, Penny. It might be good for him to go home."

When we got him there, Jeremy cried while we ate. He still

didn't have an appetite so the nose hose (as we called the tube extending through his nose to his stomach) had to stay in place, dripping precious vitamins and high energy liquid food to help his little body heal itself. Charity and my nieces eyed Jeremy curiously. "Why does Jerem' have that thing in his nose, Mommy?" Charity asked. "Jeremy doesn't like it. Jeremy wants to be home—sleep in his own bed."

Jackie had prepared a wonderful Thanksgiving meal. The turkey was moist and hot; the dressing smelled of sage and thyme, and her hot whipped potatoes were covered with rich brown gravy. Although the food she arranged on our plates looked lovely, I barely noticed the taste as I ate. Jeremy's whimpering controlled me.

Jackie, being a registered nurse, understood well the dangers of infection. She held Jeremy as we ate, wearing a face mask and a clean gown over her clothes to protect Jeremy.

"Eeeeeh! Eeeeeh!" Jeremy moaned rhythmically.

"We better get him back to the hospital," Tim said. "He's really uncomfortable."

We hugged Charity tightly before leaving her again. "Honey, we love you. It's going to be okay. Mommy and Daddy have to help the doctors take care of Jeremy for awhile and then we'll all be together again." Charity stood in the window seat waving as we backed from the driveway. I felt torn between my children.

I held Jeremy, one arm wrapped carefully around his body, the other holding two pillows which supported his legs. His cries as we drove the now familiar route back to the hospital reached into my heart. On the brink of panic, I cried, "Tim!"

"We'll be there in another five minutes, Hon. I don't want to drive too fast when you have to hold him like that. Just hang on. We'll get there."

The fifteen minute trip seemed endless.

The day after Thanksgiving, Jeremy went to surgery again. This time the surgical procedure would be to graft skin to Jeremy's legs from areas of his body that hadn't been burned.

The donor sites where the good skin would be taken would be put into a machine and meshed so it could be stretched to cover more burned area. The donor sites, Dr. Ahrenholz further explained, would be extremely painful because only the top layer of skin is taken. Since the nerve endings are left exposed, it is functionally a second-degree burn, he noted.

He warned us there could be scarring from the procedure. I asked if he could use skin from Jeremy's back and chest for donor sites and not shave his head as was often done. I had seen the patients in the Center whose heads had been shaved; their hair, now, the length of day old whisker stubble. To me, it seemed the ultimate indignity. I wanted Jeremy's head, at least, to look normal.

Dr. Ahrenholz only said, "We'll try, but we won't know for sure until we get in there."

We signed papers giving permission for the operation. Our neighbor, Jenny, again assisting, had assured us she'd have the operating room nice and warm. We stood beside the gurney which would carry Jeremy to surgery. He looked so small and innocent. *Why, God? Why Punky?*

"Okay," the orderly said, "Let's take him down. You two can wait in the family room."

"Just a minute," I said. I quickly wrote a note and attached it to Jeremy's sleeve. Tim and I bent down to kiss him just as they started to wheel him off.

"What was that all about?" Tim asked.

"I just wrote, 'Please don't take my hair.' Think they'll know who wrote it?"

"I'm sure they'll never guess," Tim said dryly.

While we waited for Jeremy to return from surgery Ann came into the family room in street clothes.

She leaned close to me and whispered, "I need my money. Please go in my room and get it? It's in the top drawer of my night stand."

"Ann, I can't do that. They'll think I'm stealing from you. I'll go ask Marie to help you find it, though."

"No!" Her eyes blazed. "Don't tell anyone!" Then in a pleading tone she whispered, "Please. Just go get it. I'm on a pass and they won't give me my money."

My heart was wrenched. I knew she thought I was her friend. If I betrayed her trust, would she ever trust me again?

Torn, I hesitantly consented, "Okay, I'll go see what I can do. But I'll have to tell them you sent me."

I walked in through the swinging doors of the Burn Center and said, "Marie, Ann wants some money out of her drawer. She says she's on a pass and needs it."

"She's leaving of her own volition, Penny. She's confused. Anyway, she doesn't have any money in there."

"Where will she go?"

"We don't know. There's nothing we can do to keep Ann here if she chooses to leave. We just hope it won't be too late."

"What do you mean—too late?"

"It's mighty cold today. If she doesn't find shelter her grafts will fall off and she'll have to start all over."

My mind pictured what starting all over would mean to Ann. "Marie, do you think I can stop her?"

"You can try, but it probably won't do any good."

I couldn't convince Ann to stay. As the minutes and hours ticked on my thoughts were of Jeremy in surgery, and Ann . . . out in the cold. Ann's words, "Andy looked a lot like Jeremy," haunted me. Maybe we shouldn't have encouraged her to talk about her son. Maybe it was too soon for her to remember.

The hours dragged as we waited for Jeremy. Nearly five hours later, we finally saw them wheel him by. Relief filled us. At least the surgery was over.

Dr. Ahrenholz seemed optimistic. "It went well," he said. "His legs looked really clean."

Maybe Jeremy's legs wouldn't look like the pictures I avoided seeing every day as I walked down the hall. Maybe Punky's legs would look normal again.

We went in to see Jeremy after they'd settled him. He was still sleeping from the anesthesia. Blessed sleep. If only they could let him sleep through this whole ordeal.

Jeremy's legs were covered with elastomer dressings, a brown plastic foam that ballooned out, protecting the sensitive graft sites. A special synthetic material was placed over his donor sites. The material looked like heavy Saran wrap. The donor sites were red and bloody. Claudia said, "We are medicating Jeremy as much as we can. We will do everything possible to minimize the pain."

My stomach turned as I looked at Jeremy's bloody back and the upper thigh they had used for donor skin, but I was grateful they hadn't used skin from his arms or shaved his head.

By evening Jeremy was running a high temperature. "Is it normal to run a temp' after this kind of surgery?" I asked.

"No, it's not," a nurse said. "We don't like it. It could be a sign of infection or he could have a virus. We don't know yet what it's from."

Later I shared my concern with Tim. "The staff seems worried. If only we hadn't taken him home for Thanksgiving." I twisted the Kleenex I was holding into a fine point. "Maybe then, he wouldn't be sick now."

Jeremy had been moved to a new room. He had four male roommates. One was Al, Madge's husband. Tim and I took turns standing hunched over Jeremy's bed. He clung to us, both arms wielded tightly around our necks. When Tim's back became sore from bending, I pried Jeremy's fingers loose. He grabbed me and hung on as if for life itself.

"He's so scared isn't he?" Al said, watching the pitiful ritual from his nearby bed. "And such a dear little boy. Don't you worry. I"ll watch over him tonight when you go home."

Just before we left that evening I checked with the nurses to find out if anyone had heard from Ann.

"Didn't you hear?" they asked.

I shook my head.

"She jumped off a bridge into the Mississippi."

"Oh God! No!"

The nurse hastened to add, "She's okay. The police were following and got to her before her grafts were damaged. She's safe in the psych ward right now. From now on she'll just come down here for baths and therapy."

Jeremy had to wear the elastomer splints for a few days before his graft sites would be uncovered. For those days he didn't have to have baths. Also, for those days he couldn't move. Grafted skin is very sensitive although the elastimers helped to protect the graft sites. Every precaution was taken to see that nothing jeopardized his grafts from taking.

The doctors postponed the date the elastimers would be removed since Jeremy had been sick. "An extra day or two might give the grafts more time to take," they said.

In spite of all our questions regarding God's intervention in our lives, we continued to ask people to pray that Jeremy's grafts would take. Surely with thousands praying all over the world, as well as the relatively low incidence of grafts "not taking," God would ensure this much for our son.

Occasional premonitions of failure would slip through my consciousness. Jeremy continued to run a fever, a possible sign of infection in the graft sites. Although we hoped it was just a virus we didn't know.

The fourth morning after surgery, I walked into the Center and was told to go wait in the family room. "The doctors are in now removing Jeremy's elastomers," the nurse said.

Darla and Madge waited with me. I called Tim, home teaching at Kids' Kottage Daycare Center, to tell him the news.

"Call back as soon as you know anything," he requested.

Time dragged. Darla and Madge both assured me that in their months in the Center everyone's grafts had taken well. Although encouraged, I remained somewhat concerned. It was taking so long. It seemed they'd been in with Jeremy at least an hour.

Finally Darla said, "It shouldn't take this long. I bet they just forgot to tell you they were done. Why don't you call in there and see?"

Quickly I dialed the number. Marie answered and after checking with the doctors said, "Come on in and Dr. Ahrenholz will talk to you."

I hurried down the hall past the grotesque pictures and the therapy rooms. Just as I reached the swinging doors opening into the Burn Center, Dr. Ahrenholz stepped out. He put his arm around me and with tears in his eyes said, "I'm sorry. I don't know what happened. They didn't take well."

"Oh God! No!"

"I'm sorry," he repeated, "We did have a small percentage of the grafts take and probably some of the skin around those areas will grow in. We'll have to wait and see."

"How soon?" My voice faltered. "How soon can you graft again?"

He quietly explained, "We can't graft until we're sure of what will take and what won't. Probably it will be two or three weeks. In the meantime we'll watch his legs closely to avoid further infection."

"But I thought Jeremy could go home in a month. How can he do that if he's not even grafted for another three weeks?"

"Jeremy won't be going home in a month. That date would have been appropriate if the grafts had taken. Now I'd guess closer to two months. Right now the important thing is to get that fever down and the graft sites cleaned up. We've already taken samples of Jeremy's donor sites and graft sites for cultures. We need to know what kind of infection he's got. That will give us more information about why his grafts didn't take."

Dr. Ahrenholz's eyes were tender as his hand touched my shoulder. "Penny, we'll need you and Tim to sign some forms for a cut-down this afternoon. It's a minor surgery which we can do in his room."

"A cut-down?" I searched his face.

"A cut-in to his jugular vein. We need to get some strong antibiotics into his system. The jugular vein is large enough to handle the strength of the antibiotic." He paused. "We need to get this infection under control."

I went in to see my son. He was crying. His hazel eyes were filled with the panic I was becoming used to seeing. When he saw me he reached out for my neck and pulled my face into his honey-blonde hair. I raged inwardly. *Dear God, here is my son! Autistic! Burned! Fighting for his life! Couldn't you even see to it that his grafts took?*

Marie, Jeremy's favorite nurse, walked in, Jeremy cried out when he saw her. She smiled, "He's getting smart, he knows who brings the owies."

Struggling to escape Jeremy's tight grip, I turned my head toward Marie. "How often does this happen? I mean that grafts don't take."

She spoke forthrightly. "It happens occasionally. It's pretty rare that this amount of the graft doesn't take, however. The doctors said this morning they are going to look into the possibility that Jeremy's handicapped condition might have something to do with it."

Rare! It seemed the story of our lives. My mind mimicked the many times doctors and teachers had sought to comfort us with, "This is an extremely rare condition." "I have never seen a more mysterious child in all my years of practice." "He is unique; he's unlike any child we've seen here." Rare! I'd settle for dull, normal, and predictable.

Remembering I needed to call Tim, I asked Marie for help in disentangling Jeremy's arms from around me. I gave him a big teddy bear we had brought from home and kissed his forehead. "It's going to be okay, Punky Boy. We'll get through this yet."

In the family room again I collapsed on the familiar green chairs and answered Darla and Madge's questions of, "Did they take?" Tears shone in Madge's eyes as I relayed to her what Dr. Ahrenholz had said.

Darla characteristically shouted, "Holy crap!" For once it didn't shock me. My feelings exactly.

When I spoke to Tim, he, too, was incredulous. The beliefs we had about God intervening seemed again to crash with reality. Speaking to Tim upset any semblance of composure I'd managed so far to maintain. I sat and cried, holding my head in my hands. It felt good, to taste the salty tears, to release some of the pent-up tensions of the past days, to be real with Madge and Darla . . . who really did understand.

Claudia, and Cliff, the Burn Center social worker, walked in and asked, "Would you like group in here today?"

Darla said, "Sure. Why not?"

I had forgotten all about group. Once a week the families of the burn patients met with Cliff and Claudia to discuss feelings about what was happening to their loved one. Ordinarily, it was hard for me to open up in that kind of setting. Today it seemed impossible. Darla sat down beside me, wrapping her arms around my shoulders. "There, there. Poor little mommy. Your baby's gonna be all right," she crooned like an old grandmother, as I sobbed in her arms.

Cliff and Claudia looked on as they watched Darla comfort me. Madge quietly handed me tissues, tears shining in her eyes. I knew Darla and Madge understood my pain. They had been there. True to my Scandinavian heritage, however, I was uncomfortable letting professionals see my brokenness. I felt emotionally naked.

Struggling to gain control of my tears, I longed to cover my raw emotions just as surely as Jeremy's raw nerve endings longed for the cover of grafted skin. I thought it ironic that neither of us had gotten the cover we so desperately wanted.

12

A Gift of Love

Jeremy had been in the Burn Center since the week before Thanksgiving. Unseasonably warm weather, with no snow on the ground, denied the fact that Christmas was now only three weeks away. *It doesn't seem like Christmas this year anyway,* I thought, as I hurried to the elevators that would carry me up to 5 East. The orange doors of the elevator slid open. Immediately the strong smell of the Burn Center overwhelmed me. Hanging my coat in the family room, I greeted Darla.

"Where's Tim?" she asked.

"At Kids' Kottage. He'll be here after he sends the kindergartners to school."

Suddenly, I noticed two Indian women sitting near her. *Oh no, not another one,* I thought. We all dreaded seeing anyone else being admitted to the Burn Center, knowing even more than they, what would lie ahead.

"Hello. I'm Penny. Do you have someone in here?"

The women appeared to be shy, but the younger answered if somewhat hesitantly. "My girl's here. This here's my ma."

"What happened?" I asked.

"Aw, she was playin' with matches, and set the bed 'un fire."

"I'm really sorry. My little boy is here too. I'm on my way to see him. Maybe I'll see you in there later."

I gowned and walked in to see Jeremy. He wasn't in his bed.

Marie came by and said, "He's in the solarium, Penny. Just finishing his breakfast."

He's eating today?"

She grinned. "Well, not much. He did take a couple spoonfuls of Cheerios this morning and he drank a little juice."

"I'll be right in, Marie. I think I'll straighten up his toys a bit first though."

I smiled as I looked at Jeremy's bed filled with stuffed animals of all description. Dozens of cuddly toys began arriving after the story was told about Jeremy clinging to our necks and how we relieved our sore backs by replacing ourselves with a teddy bear. Hundreds of cards from friends, relatives, and church members also had come—many of them colorfully wallpapering Jeremy's hospital room walls. As I lined up the animals at the end of Jeremy's bed, I looked up and read again the sign, Carole, his tutor, had made for him. It said,

JESUS LOVES YOU
PUNKY BOY!

A bouquet of multicolored balloons hung from his lamp. A large poster leaned against his bed rail with bright pictures of "Grandpa's" farm, farm animals, and our family. My mom, home at the farm, still recuperating from pneumonia, had made it for Jeremy, knowing it would help him to see the people and things he loved. To the left of his bed hung a poem called "Footprints in the Sand." I quickly finished arranging Jeremy's dresser and walked over to read it again.

> *One night I had a dream*
> *I dreamed I was walking along the beach*
> *with the Lord and*
> *Across the sky flashed scenes from my*
> *life.*
> *For each scene I noticed two sets of*
> *footprints in the sand,*
> *One belonged to me and the other to the*
> *Lord.*
> *When the last scene of my life flashed*
> *before us,*
> *I looked back at the footprints in the*
> *sand.*
> *I noticed that many times along the*
> *path of my life,*
> *There was only one set of footprints.*
> *I also noticed that it happened at the*
> *very lowest and saddest times in my life.*

*This really bothered me and I questioned
the Lord about it.
"Lord, You said that once I decided to
follow You,
You would walk with me all the way,
But I have noticed that during the most
troublesome times in my life,
There is only one set of footprints.
I don't understand why in times when I
needed You most, You should leave me."
The Lord replied, "My precious, precious
child, I love you and I would never,
never leave you during your times of
trial and suffering.
When you see only one set of footprints,
It was then that I carried you."*

—Author Unknown

Dear God, thank you for this bit of truth. At least I know You won't leave me. Please carry me today.

Marie and an aide pulled Jeremy in the little red fire engine wagon into his room. "Would you like to rock him for awhile?" Marie asked. "I'll help you get settled."

"You are such a dear, Marie. I'd love to." Marie carefully lifted Jeremy into my arms, being careful not to bump his thickly bandaged legs. She swung the "nose hose" cord around the I.V. pole connected to it, and covered us both with a fluffy white blanket. Jeremy moaned. My heart ached.

Marie said, "What's the matter, tough guy? Should we get a big pillow for your legs?" She carefully lifted Jeremy's legs and deftly shoved two fat pillows on my lap thus elevating Jeremy's legs. Jeremy whimpered again, but then lay back with a weary look on his little face.

As we rocked together I said, "Marie, how did bath time go today? Were you in with Jeremy again?"

"Yes I was. He had a lot of pain again. I spoke to the doctors and we are going to try giving him more pain medication tomorrow. Hopefully that will make him a little more comfortable. He's such a good little buddy." She sighed. "As soon as he gets out of the water, he quits screaming and looks at us as if to say, 'Oh thank you, thank you for getting me out of there.'"

"Poor baby," I said stroking Jeremy's glowing blonde hair. His eyes were fixed on mine.

Marie continued, "Lately, he even helps us as we dress him. I'll say, 'Jeremy, lift your leg,' and he'll follow my instructions right through the dressings, bandages, to the ace wrapping on his legs and back. He's a smart little guy." She paused, gazing out the window as the traffic on Interstate 94 rushed by. "I just hate to see him suffer so."

"Marie, Jeremy never used to be able to follow directions. Do you think . . . I mean, is it possible that something happened to his biochemistry when he got burned that's improving his neurological condition? We've noticed changes too. He's been looking us straight in the eye. Yesterday he was watching TV which is a miracle in itself, but the weird thing was something funny happened and he laughed. He laughed, Marie. And just at the right time."

"I'll mention it to the doctors and see what they think. It sure would be nice to think something good could come from this little guy's pain."

Later that morning I was arranging Jeremy's cards when one of the nurses sauntered in. "How's Jerem' doing today?"

"Sleeping right now. He's been crying on and off, though."

"Did you meet the Indian mother?"

"Yeah, that's sure too bad. She said her little girl was burned with matches."

"Was she still laughing?" the nurse asked with a trace of bitterness.

"No. She seemed pretty calm about it all though. Why? Was she hysterical when they brought her little girl in? I'll never forget how upset I was the day Jeremy was burned."

"She wasn't hysterical at all. She thought it was funny. She wasn't even home when Shannie was burned. All three of her young children were home alone. Shannie started playing with matches in her bed and the whole bed ignited."

"Oh no," I exclaimed.

Jeremy shifted on his bed. "Owwwiiiiee!" he cried.

"It's okay, Honey. No owies for you. Mommie's just talking about another little girl who's got bad owies." I turned back to the nurse, "Do you think she'll make it?"

"It's hard to say, Penny. Young children and older people are the ones we worry about most. Kids have so much growing to do that scarring can be a real problem. Young adults seem to have the easiest time recovering."

"Did the other kids call an ambulance when Shannie got burned? Did the house burn down?" I shot my questions at her.

"No, they got the fire out. It was below zero that night but apparently the kids couldn't stand her screaming. As I understand it, and we don't know all the details, they threw her out in the snow. She was out there all night before anyone came home to find her."

"You've got to be kidding!" I gasped.

"Actually it probably saved her life—if she makes it. She's burned on fifty percent of her body. The cutest little thing you ever could see, though."

Later, I mused about what the nurse had said as I rocked my Punky. He lay immobile in my arms. Afraid to move for the pain, I supposed. I sang to him half-expecting to hear his sweet little voice join me on "Jesus Loves Me," but he just stared into my eyes. It occurred to me that I hadn't heard him sing or even hum since he'd been burned.

"You poor baby, you haven't had much to sing about, have you?" I said, as I stroked his head gently. Jeremy gazed into my eyes as if trying to tell me what it was like at bath time.

Oh dear God. Help him, I whispered in his hair.

As much as I loved my son, I wondered if I would go through those baths for him even if I could have. I wondered, would I want to die instead? The fleeting thoughts filled me with guilt. How could I think I was so much different from the Indian mother?

Jeremy gradually closed his eyes and drifted into a peaceful sleep. I carefully put him in his bed, again elevating his legs, trying not to notice the oozing liquid seeping through his bandages and ace wrappings. Covering him gently, I started when a nurse tapped me on the shoulder and said, "Someone's here to see you, but it's not visiting hours yet. You can just talk to him by the nurses station if you don't want to re-gown."

"Thanks." I looked out the door and saw it was our good friend, Neil Stavem, from the Beta Sunday school class. Neil and his wife Shari were involved in a Christian ministry in St. Paul. I was really glad to see him. The minutes ticked by slowly on days when no one came to visit us.

"Hi, Penny. How's it going?" Neil asked.

"Okay, I guess," I responded. "Can you believe this place? You're lucky it isn't visiting hours so you don't have to get into all this garb."

Neil said, "Yeah, I can see that. I can't stay too long anyway. I just wanted to bring this card over and let you know we're thinking of you."

"Well, thank you, Neil. We appreciate that a lot. It's friends like you that keep us going."

"It's so hard to understand why things like this happen." Tears rimmed his eyes.

"I guess if we've learned anything from this, Neil, it's that there is no reason. Things just happen. At first I couldn't believe God let it happen. I mean, we'd prayed every day for protection for Jeremy. And . . . he obviously had, 'more than he could bear' already." Making imaginary quotations with my fingers, I loosely quoted the verse I had grown up believing to mean that nothing would happen one couldn't handle.

"That's for sure." Neil retorted. "You all have."

"And so have a lot of the other people in this burn center, Neil. The easy answers just don't fit."

"How are you and Tim putting it together, Penny? What does make sense now?"

I let out a deep breath, pushing the surgical cap covering my hair back from where it drooped on my forehead. "Mostly we know what we don't believe anymore. It's going to take lots of time to put it all together. I guess we're wondering if it's God plan to intervene routinely in this world's circumstances . . . to interfere with the free will He gives humans."

"I guess that's a question I've wrestled with too."

"Maybe that's something we can explore together. It used to seem kind of like mental gymnastics when Tim and I studied the problem of evil at Oak Hills Bible College. Now it's like, I have to know."

When Neil left, I sat next to Jeremy's bed and turned over the envelope he'd handed me. I felt troubled by their financial situation as I opened the card. I knew that Neil and his wife Shari were living on a tight budget. In fact, in order for them to continue in their ministry they had recently decided to sell their home. I sighed now, remembering, as I read the letter Shari had written.

It just doesn't seem fair that a burden such as this had to be added to Jeremy's young life. I have started a letter so many times before but I can't seem to get much written before I start crying and just end up praying for you instead. Please accept this gift of money as a small part of the love we feel for your family. It won't go far with all the bills you must have, but use it for anything you have an immediate need for.
With love, Shari

From out of the envelope fell a crisp one-hundred dollar bill. I was shocked and humbled by the generosity and love that motivated Neil and Shari's gift to us. But it wasn't right. We just couldn't accept that money knowing how they were struggling financially. Although one of Jeremy's former roommates had gone home to find the hospital had placed a lien on his farm, we were hopeful our insurance company would eventually come through for most of Jeremy's hospital expenses. Jeremy getting better was our main concern. Money we could always come by.

Quickly I dialed Shari's number. "Shari, this is Penny."

"Penny! How are you? Has Neil been by yet?" Shari asked sweetly.

"I'm fine, Shari. Neil just left and that's kind of why I'm calling," I sighed. "Shari, we just can't take that money. Your giving it to us is something I will never forget, but you all need it more than we do."

Shari's voice sounded firm as she told me, "You and Tim have lots of extra expenses now with gas and eating at the hospital. We won't take that money back. It's not very much, but it's the only way we know how to help you."

Later when Tim met me at the hospital for supper, I told him about Neil's visit and the card and money he'd left.

"We can't take that," Tim declared. "They are the last people who can afford to give it."

"I know, Honey. I already called Shari and she wouldn't hear of our returning it. I know it's hard to do, but this time I think we need to accept this as the gift of love it was meant to be."

It was Tim's turn to spend the next morning with Jeremy at the hospital. After sending the children in Kids' Kottage Daycare Center off to kindergarten for the afternoon, I hurried to meet him and Jeremy in the Burn Center. Driving to Ramsey Hospital had become such a common routine I drove almost without thinking. It seemed as if the car knew that was the way to go. And in fact it was the only place our little red Opel traveled. Tim and I ate at the Center or close by. If we stopped for groceries for Kids' Kottage it was on the way home from the hospital. Pulling into the Ramsey parking ramp, I stopped the car and ran to the elevator that would carry me to 5 East and the long corridor leading to the Center.

"How did Jeremy's bath go today?" I asked Tim after gowning and then kissing Jeremy as he lay sleeping in his daddy's arms.

"I don't know, Hon. They've had a couple of new admits today. I haven't gotten a chance to ask anyone."

"Ask anyone what?" Marie said brightly as she swept into Jeremy's room.

"How bath time went for Jerem' today?" I repeated.

Marie frowned as she answered. "He didn't have much pain today. We gave him more medication than we ever have before. He was so out of it that he could have drowned. We'll never give him that much again." She paused. "This is the first day he's had any comfort at all and then it was too much."

"We really appreciate your concern over Jeremy's pain," Tim said.

"Our pain-reliever use per patient falls in the top ten percent nationally," Marie stated, "Even so we still can't control all the pain."

"Well, we're really glad Jeremy is here. People have been telling us this is the best burn center in the nation."

Marie laughed, "I'm not going to argue with you."

Tim and I were ready to leave to work the afternoon shift at Kids' Kottage when the resident doctor following Jeremy's case stopped us in the hall. "You two leaving?"

"We'll be back soon. We just have to go work for a couple of hours," Tim said.

"I just wanted to talk to you about Jeremy's neurological condition. We're watching it very closely. Marie mentioned to us at staff meeting today that he is showing a longer attention span and is actually helping dress his burns. We don't know, but it's possible one of the meds we're giving him for pain is helping his other problems."

My stomach lurched. "Really! Is it something we could keep him on?" I asked as hope began to dawn again.

"We don't know yet what it is that's helping him," he cautioned. "If it's a med, we probably can. It could also be related to his body chemistry being changed from being burned. . . ." He hesitated, pushing his glasses higher on his nose, "And it could just be the pain is so intense that it forces his neurological system to focus on what's happening."

Choosing to believe the former, I practically skipped to our little red Opel. Maybe, just maybe, Jeremy would get better after all!

13

"God With Us"

My hands moved swiftly, placing the paper pattern on the colorful felt, then cutting and gluing each shape to the burlap Advent calendar. Occasionally, I glanced at Jeremy sleeping on the hospital bed beside me. My mother had sent the Advent calendar kit complete with felt patterns and Advent messages ready to be cut and glued. "It will be good for you to have something to do when you sit with Jeremy at the hospital," she said.

As I traced the thirty-one days of December on the calendar, I noted that several of those days had already passed.

Time seemed a blur. This Christmas season held no enchantment for us. Instead, we waited wearily for the time when Jeremy could have his third, and hopefully, final surgery. Christmas, for once, was low on our list of priorities.

Each day, since the uncovering of Jeremy's graft sites had revealed infection and rotting tissue as a result of his grafts not taking, Jeremy had endured excruciating pain in the baths. Normally, a burn is covered with meshed, grafted skin within a few days of the injury. The covering of the nerve endings helps minimize the pain, particularily at bath time, but Jeremy's nerve endings were not covered yet. The doctors needed to be certain the infection and rotted skin were completely gone before regrafting. Our one bright spot was the hope that one of the medications Jeremy was taking might help to treat his autistic condition.

Carefully tracing a Christmas star, my thoughts turned to Al and Madge. It seemed so lonely without them in the Burn Center, even though they'd been gone just a week.

"Hi there!" Claudia walked in with a big smile on her pretty

Scandinavian face. "What are you up to?"

"My mom sent this stuff. She was probably trying to keep me out of your hair," I smirked.

"Your family and friends have been so supportive, Penny. By the way, here's another gift that arrived while you were down for lunch."

"They didn't say who it was from?" I asked, turning the small package in my hand.

"No, a young woman just brought it in. I believe there's a card though."

"Here, it is. . . . It's from Central Payment Union. I don't believe it."

"Who's that?" Claudia asked.

"It's a government agency we work with to service poor children in our daycare center. I don't even know how they knew about the accident. This is incredible."

"Look's like Punky is waking up," Claudia said. "Why don't you open it for him."

Carefully, I opened the festive Christmas paper. Inside was a digital musical phone. "Look, Claudia. This is about the only kind of toy Jeremy ever shows any interest in."

Claudia looked around the room noticing the many stuffed animals, balloons, tractors, posters, and cards. "This is one little boy who is really loved." She hesitated. "Some people wouldn't treat their handicapped child this way, you know."

"Jeremy is ours and we love him just as he is; any parent would," I insisted.

"I know that's how you feel. He is a special boy." She nodded toward the nurse's station. "But we all are just amazed at how everyone in your family and all of your friends care so much about him too."

"Each person with life should be treated with as much respect as any other," I said softly.

"Eeeeeh!" Jeremy cried, rolling his head around to search for me.

"Mommy's here, Punky Boy." Sitting gingerly on the edge of the bed, I turned back to Claudia. "He's been through so much, hasn't he?"

Nodding, she replied, "I'll never forget, as long as I live, when Jeremy came in here."

Surprised, I asked, "Why? You've worked here for a long time, haven't you? You must have seen everything in that time."

"Jeremy was different." She sighed, remembering. "We didn't even know he was coming till he was downstairs in ER."

"Why? I was in the ambulance. I heard them make the call to the hospital."

"Well, no one called us. We didn't have a doctor's order for morphine and so we had to debride without it. Jeremy just kept screaming and screaming. I've never seen anyone look so terrified. He couldn't tell us what he was thinking. He couldn't understand what we told him . . . . I'll never forget it."

My eyes felt hot and a rock filled my stomach as I asked quietly, "You mean you took his skin off without morphine?"

"We had no choice, Penny. We had to get the damaged tissue off as soon as possible to lessen the chance of infection. We are absolutely not allowed to administer morphine without a doctor's order."*

Silently I nodded my head, knowing they'd done all they could and yet I felt angry, not at Claudia or the staff, but at the corruption of humankind that made such policing of morphine a necessity.

"Claudia, will you help me get Jeremy in my lap. I think I'd like to rock him for awhile."

That entire afternoon I played the Christmas tape Jeremy's Auntie Marilyn had made him. Each time the carol, "Emmanuel, Emmanuel, His name is called Emmanuel" played softly from the recorder, something deep within me stirred and tears would fall on the burlap Advent calender on which I worked.

Yes, God is with us! Emmanuel! Maybe that is what Christmas is really about.

The next day Tim stayed with Jeremy while I worked at Kids' Kottage Daycare Center. Taking advantage of the couple of hours all of the children were in school, I did some Christmas baking, just in case we decided to celebrate.

As I waited for the chocolate reindeer to bake, I opened the stack of mail. More cards and letters had come. Each made us feel so special, so loved.

I realized that Jeremy's being burned had brought me to a level of desperation I had never before known. Now I was also experiencing a level of love and care beyond anything I'd ever known.

---

*Dr. Ahrenholz informed me, when reviewing this manuscript, that the standing orders have been changed so no patient is debrided without morphine if he has pain.

Perhaps it was there all the time, but through this accident people were more able to show they cared. Was God caring for us through people?

From among the dozens of cards a postcard sized envelope fell into my lap. The buzzer rang just then, signaling my cookies were ready.

"It'll have to wait," I said to no one in particular. "Gotta get those cookies."

A short time later, I opened the unimpressive envelope. A postcard folded in half almost hid the check inside it. Curious now, I read the message.

The Lord has given us some money to share with some of His children who are depending on Him. We weren't sure who to give it to. Then on a rare shopping trip to St. Paul we ran into Linda and Dave . They told us about you. Lyning and I agreed you are the ones. Thank you, Lord, for telling us to be a part of what you are doing in the lives of others. Amen.

Lyning! I had worked with Lyning in the kitchen at Oak Hills Bible College almost ten years ago. We had seen them only twice since. How sweet of them to send us money. I opened the check and gulped as I read the amount: $400.00. *Dear God, you do work in people's lives don't you. Why else would people share with someone else what was rightfully theirs?*

The day proved to be full of surprises. My brother-in-law, Bob, stopped by with a Christmas tree he had purchased for us up north. "Just in case you decide to celebrate," he said.

Then just before the Kids' Kottage children arrived home from school the phone rang. "Hello, this is Santa Claus," the voice on the other side said.

"Come off it, John. I know it's you," I said, laughing.

"This isn't John. It's Santa Claus," the voice insisted. "I've called to see if anyone will be home in the morning. I have a delivery to make for the family of Jeremy Giesbrecht."

"John, you don't have to do that. I mean someone will be home, but really you and Marie have done so much already."

"Look, this isn't John. I don't know who you think this is. I'm someone from Trinity Church and I want to bring over the makings of a turkey dinner for your family for Christmas."

I was speechless. "Hey, are you still there, Penny?" he asked.

"Yes, I just don't know what to say. I thought you were John Peterson from church. Who are you?"

"Let's just say I'm, uh, Santa Claus, okay?"

"Santa Claus?"

"Yes."

"Thank you."

After closing the Kids' Kottage that night I drove as fast as was safe toward Ramsey Hospital where Tim and Jeremy were waiting.

As I turned onto the freeway I thought about Charity. I missed her so even though I knew she was in good hands at my parents' house. It had been almost three weeks now since we'd seen her. By Christmas, I hoped, she'd come home.

Right now, however, I was anxious to see my little boy and share with Tim all that had happened. I hopped from the car and ran against the whipping wind to the glass entrance door. As I rounded the corridor I noticed the elevator door just about to close. "Could you hold it please?" I asked.

"Sure can, Penny," Al said.

"Al! Madge! Are you here for your check-up?" I asked as we exchanged hugs in the crowded elevator.

"Yeah, we're all done. We were just on our way up to see Jeremy."

"So am I. Tim's been here all day and I was at Kids' Kottage. Have you seen Steve and Darla?"

"Yes we did. Steve is up and walking around. He may be able to leave by the New Year, the doctors said. How's Punky Boy doing?"

"He's having a hard time with his baths. Not having his nerve endings covered makes it pretty painful."

"I remember so little of my first two weeks here," Al said. "But I do remember that the baths were really an ordeal until they grafted. After that it was so much better."

"Yeah, that's what the nurses tell us, too. We hope they'll be grafting soon. Jeremy's already been without a covering on his legs for a month now. They say they have to be sure all the tissue is prepared for the grafts. I think they hope to reharvest his donor sites too. If they wait long enough, they'll be able to."

Later that evening, after having encouraged everyone in the Burn Center with their visits, Al and Madge came into Jeremy's room to say goodbye.

Al stood shuffling his bedroom-slipper-clad feet to help alleviate the soreness from his burns. He pushed his fingers through his thick gray hair as he said, "You know, the hardest part about leaving the hospital was knowing I was leaving Jeremy behind. I think of him a hundred times a day."

His eyes filled with tears and his voice broke as he pointed to

Jeremy's bed. "If I could lay down in this bed and go through it all over again for him, I would."

I shared this story in our annual Christmas letter, telling friends and relatives how the spirit of Christmas had been demonstrated to us by our Catholic brother, Al.

I ended the letter with this sentence, "You see the spirit of Christmas is everywhere. Yes, Emmanuel, 'God with us' even in the St. Paul Ramsey Burn Center."

A few nights later Tim and I came home about eleven and found a note on the door. "Free Spirit was here to carol. Sorry we missed you. If you get home soon, call us at Wallaces'." Beside the note was a brown box filled with presents, cookies, and baked goodies.

"Oh Tim, my junior high choir kids at church. They remembered us." We called the Wallaces' number, hoping to catch at least some and thank them for their love.

Although only a few were still there they hopped into a car and came over with their sponsor, Scott Wallace. The kids and I made popcorn in the daycare center while Tim and Scott visited upstairs.

Scott's daughter, Karen, asked, "Penny, why do you think this happened to Jeremy? It doesn't seem fair."

"I think it just happened, Karen. I don't think there was any special reason or purpose. We live in a fallen world where bad things happen to everybody, even to believers."

We shared together until after midnight. The special openness, unique to junior highers, touched me deeply. They ministered to me in a way many Christian adults had not been able to do.

One Friday, shortly before Christmas, I sat with my auto harp at Jeremy's bedside singing every song I could remember. Jeremy didn't cry as long as I sang. Often he would grab my hand and put it back on the harp when a song was finished. As I began "Away in the Manger" for the third time that afternoon, Pastor Hart walked in, flashing the boyish smile that always managed to make him look much younger than his forty-five years.

"How are you doing, Penny?" he asked putting his arm lightly around my shoulder.

"Jeremy is having a fairly good day today. You look awfully tired, though."

"I guess I am, Penny. I just came back from the World Missions Board meeting. We don't have enough money to pay for supplies overseas this year. We have only enough to pay missionary salaries. I'm glad we can do that." He sighed deeply. "It just hurts to know their work will be so limited without money to facilitate it."

I knew Pastor Hart's committment to missions ran deep. He and Marlene had been missionaries in the Philippines for many years before returning to the States.

Late the following Monday afternoon, we received word Pastor Hart had suffered a severe heart attack. We ached for him and his family. They had done so much for us and now I longed to reach out to them in some way.

That evening at home, we arranged some of the chocolate reindeer and other goodies I'd baked on a plate that said, "Let's be friends." On top of the plate was a card that read, "As you bore our burdens, so now we bear yours." I felt badly I didn't have something more to bring, but we hoped at least they'd know we loved them and were thinking of them.

The Beta Sunday School class cared for us in many ways. One of the most practical was the two evenings a dozen guys came over to help Tim sheetrock the new area of our house addition. Tim had hopes of finishing the dusty job before we brought Jeremy home from the hospital.

One of those "work nights" I went to the hospital alone while Tim stayed home to help. A new family from out of town was in the family room when I arrived. Their newlywed daughter, Debbie and son-in-law, Mike, had just been severely burned in a car crash when a drunk driver hit their car. As the evening progressed, Debbie's parents decided to stay overnight in St. Paul, since surgery for the couple had been scheduled the following day.

Impulsively I volunteered, "Hey, we're still building our house, but if you don't mind a mess and sleeping on the floor, come sleep at our house."

"A building mess would make us feel right at home. We've been adding on to our house for years," they replied.

So it was settled. Debbie's parents followed me home. As we pulled up to our cedar house a dozen cars reminded me the Beta crew was still sheetrocking. I would have to introduce Deb's parents to them. I let out a low whistle. I didn't know their names.

I got out of my car and walked to our guests' truck. "Our friends are still here sheet-rocking," I said, "I just realized I don't know your names. If I walk in, and don't know who you are when I introduce you, I will never live it down."

Dave and Mavis Jorde introduced themselves, laughing at my dilemma. They were our kind of people.

Just a week before Christmas we received a letter from Al:

*We made it home okay and we think of you all the time.
We are praying harder than ever for healing for Jeremy and
strength for his mom and dad and sister during this difficult
time and yes we cry at times when we think of how patiently
he suffers. It makes me want to do something. I feel so
helpless here. I have been wondering and worrying about
whether he has enough donor site skin left for grafting and I
want you to know that if it would be possible that I could be
a donor for him, I would come immediately. I am not kidding. I have a lot of area left on my tummy and I seem to
heal well and I would consider it a real honor to be able to be
a donor for Jeremy, rather than have any more areas of his
body opened . . . .*

Tim and I were overcome by Al's letter. We knew that it was
not possible to use someone else's skin for donor sites.

The fact that Al would consider it, knowing even more than we
the tormenting pain that followed donor skin being lifted, humbled us.

That evening we were standing at the nurses station discussing
Al's letter when the phone rang.

"It's for you," the nurse said. "Go ahead and take it here if you
like."

"Tim, have you talked to the doctors yet?" Al asked. "I'm
ready to come right now."

Tim told him, "Al, no one can be the donor for Jeremy, but the
fact that you offered is the greatest gift anyone could ever receive.
You stay home with your family in North Dakota and have a
wonderful Christmas. We love you."

Two days before Christmas the doctors said, "Christmas is for
kids. We aren't going to graft again until after Christmas. You'll
be able to take Jeremy home for a few hours at a time during the
holidays."

We were suddenly in need of all the food "Santa Claus" and
other friends had brought—"just in case we should decide to
celebrate."

My family made plans to celebrate with us the day before
Christmas Eve. I stayed home to cook the turkey while Tim,
Mom and Dad, and the rest of my family went to the hospital to
pick up Jeremy and sing carols in the Center, something we'd
intended to do if we'd brought our Christmas celebration to the
hospital.

I pulled the turkey from the oven just as the door opened.

"Hi Auntie Penny!" Tracey and Benji, my niece and nephew cried.

Shaking the snow from their coats, my mom and dad, my brother, my sisters with their husbands and babies, bustled in the door. Tim came last, cautiously carrying Jeremy, bundled in so many blankets I could only see his pale face. Charity ran in circles around them. "Mommy, Mommy! Jeremy's here!"

Swinging Charity up in my arms, I leaned over and kissed Jeremy's cheek. I felt like it was really Christmas!

A reclining chair, where his legs could easily be kept elevated, made a comfortable bed for Jeremy. Again, we answered sundry questions from Jeremy's young cousins about the "nose hose" and Jeremy's owie legs. Jeremy cried some, but seemed to quiet when one of us, sitting next to him, would stroke his forehead. Tim stayed close to Jeremy while my mother and sisters helped me put the finishing touches on the dinner.

Standing back, I looked at the huge table laden with food. The turkey skin looked crisp and brown, the meat succulent. The red of the cranberry sauce stood in sharp contrast to the hot whipped potatoes next to it. Yellow squash, green peas, and rich brown gravy surrounded relish trays in a colorful circle. Hot apple pies sat on the counter waiting to be served.

Oh, it was good to be home! Although Jeremy was still a very sick little boy, he was alive and he was home. We were a family!

After our Christmas dinner we gathered in the family room of the daycare center. Dad carried Jeremy's easy chair next to the Christmas tree so he could see. Jeremy watched quietly all the Christmas activities and only occasionally cried, "Eeeehhhh," carefully moving his skinny legs an inch or two.

Charity stood near her brother, so glad to be home herself for the first time in three weeks. "It's okay, Punky. We love you," she assured him. Then turning to Tim: "Daddy, can I sit next to my brother? He's lonesome for me."

"Kids how would you like to be in the Christmas story tonight?" I asked.

"Yeah!" they shouted jumping up and down excitedly.

While sitting in the Burn Center, I had read a story of a woman with terminal cancer, who had given a Christmas pageant to her family as a gift.

I adapted the idea for my family. We used a doll to represent Baby Jesus. Charity and her cousins alternately played the roles of Joseph, Mary, shepherds, and angels. Narrating the story, I stopped often, as we sang together the corresponding carols of Christmas.

The tree lights twinkled as we concluded our first family Christmas pageant singing, "Emmanuel, Emmanuel, His name is called Emmanuel."

14

". . . Going Home at Last"

Jeremy's third burn surgery was scheduled right after Christmas. Since he had had an allergic reaction to the morphine the last time, or at least we suspected that, this time he wore a note down to surgery reading, "Morphine Allergy."

We rose at dawn to accompany Punky to the operating room. We were feeling less optimistic this third surgery. After all, we had hoped that each of the first two surgeries would be the final one.

At the door to the operating room, we squeezed Jeremy's fingers, hoping this would finally be the last trek we made together to OR.

"Go on up to the family room. We'll call you there and tell you when he'll be back in the Burn Center," the receptionist told us.

Once again we waited, fully expecting the five hour wait we had experienced twice before. The time passed slowly. We had long since read the few magazines in the family room. Off and on, family members of patients in the Burn Center drifted in to chat. Everyone knew Jeremy was in surgery. They were all concerned.

About three hours after we had left Jeremy the phone rang in the family room. It was Julie, a Christian nurse whom we'd grown fond of, "Penny, we just got a call from OR. They asked that the entire family of Jeremy Giesbrecht come down to surgery right away."

"Why? What's wrong?"

"What's happening?" Tim questioned, his eyes registering surprise.

Quickly I mouthed to Tim, Julie's words.

Julie sounded alarmed. "Wait for me. I'll be right there. I'm going with you."

In the elevator going down Julie said, "Remember, God is good."

I felt like saying, "That is not the issue here. God will be good, no matter what happens to Jeremy," but instead asked, "This is not routine is it, Julie?"

She shook her head, just as the elevator doors opened. Rushing to the receptionist, Julie said, "Jeremy Giesbrecht's family is here."

"Okay," the girl said cooly. "The doctor will be with them shortly. They can wait in there." She pointed to a small room off the main reception area.

Julie demanded, "What's going on? Why were they called here?"

"I don't know. Just wait for the doctor."

"Julie led us to the room and began to pray, "Dear God, We know all things are in your hands. We ask that Jeremy would be okay. Prepare us for whatever is ahead. Amen."

I felt like a piece of driftwood . . . old and hollow. *Punky must be dead. Oh God! He must be dead.*

Tim and I sat in silence, holding hands for several minutes. His hand was cold and damp. He stared straight ahead. I was afraid to say aloud what I most feared.

When the doctor strode in I stood up. "Is he—?"

Before my question was stated he declared, "He's just fine. The surgery went well and was over much sooner than we'd expected. I think this time it's going to be different."

God! He's O.K.! Jeremy's alive!

Slowly, we walked back to the Burn Center. My legs felt like mush. Only Tim's strong arm encircling my shoulders held me up. Tim's arm felt damp; his muscles were tense. As the elevator whizzed to 5 East my stomach lurched. I felt as if I'd been riding an emotional roller coaster.

Julie bubbled, "Isn't God good? I told you, God was good!"

I didn't acknowledge her words. I was too numb to feel anything.

Tim spoke with a deliberate slowness, "Julie, will you please find out what in the world happened in there? I never want anyone to go through what we just did."

"Sure, Tim." She squeezed his arm. "I'll talk to the doctors today."

The Burn Center had been abuzz at the unusual call for Jeremy's entire family to go to OR immediately, and met us joyfully as they learned their fears were unfounded.

As is so often true in life, even in our darkest moments, we are sometimes, "surprised by joy," as C.S. Lewis coined the term. The trauma of Jeremy's third surgery was followed by one of those joyful occasions when Tim's parents and two sisters came from Winnipeg to be with us for New Year's.

It was wonderful to have family members able to take turns sitting in the Burn Center with Jeremy. Since only two could visit at a time we brought our Scrabble game to pass the time while we waited in the family room.

"Q-u-a-f-f, 50 points," Viv, my sister-in-law, triumphed.

"What does quaff mean? I bet it's not in the dictionary," I accused. I pointed to the outdated *Webster's*, "But then, nothing's in this dictionary. We'll let it go."

"It is a word. It means to drink or ingest. I used it on an insurance form at work last week," she smirked.

"All right, we believe you," Tim's youngest sister Marilyn chimed in. "Your turn, Dad, maybe you can do something off of Viv's Q."

Tim walked into the Burn Center family room. "You guys fighting again? Penny must be playing. She has no mercy when it comes to Scrabble. Check every word you're not sure of. That dictionary is almost always on my side."

"Sure," I retorted, "That dictionary is on the side of all the illiterate. Ninety percent of the words in the English language can't be found in there."

Tim jabbed me playfully. He seemed more relaxed than in days, now that his family was here for the weekend.

"Mom's with Jeremy. Why don't you go in for awhile now and I'll take your place in the Scrabble game."

"Charity, do you want to go to the bathroom before Mommy goes to see Jeremy?" I asked.

"Auntie Mar-lon will take me," she responded firmly.

Laughing, I said, "Okay, Auntie Mar-lon will take you then." Marilyn had been staying with us for a couple of weeks, helping care for Charity and assisting at Kids' Kottage Daycare Center. I was thankful Charity and she had developed such a close bond.

I gowned and hurried into Punky's room. After hugging my son I turned to Tim's mom. "Grandma, why don't you go and get some tea. You've been with Punky a lot today."

"Okay. He looks like he's going to soon fall asleep anyway."

I stood by the bed petting Jeremy as I watched Tim's mother

leave. She was getting older. This was hard on them too.

Jeremy went to sleep. I was thankful for he had been having a tough day. Rocking in a big wooden rocker, I picked up a novel someone had brought for me to read. Reading had provided a welcome respite from the intensity of life in the Burn Center. Soon my thoughts were in far away Georgia. I was a Civil War widow, struggling to survive.

"Penny, Penny."

I jerked from the reverie of my reading. "What's wrong?" I mouthed as I walked to the door. My young sister-in-law stood motioning for me to come. "Charity fell off a chair while we were playing Scrabble. It wasn't very far, but she's crying for Mommy."

"Okay, I'll come as soon as I get out of my gown and mask. Thanks for getting me, Marilyn."

Charity was sitting in her daddy's lap sobbing, "It hurts! My armie hurts!"

"Chari, what's wrong, Hon?"

"I fell down on the floor." I reached out to touch her arm.

"No, Mommy!" she screamed, "Don't touch my armie!"

"Mommy just wants to look, Honey."

"Don't touch it! It hurts!"

Tim tried to move Charity's arm. She screamed, "Owie! Don't touch it Daddy! Owie! Don't touch it!"

"Leave it alone, Tim. You're hurting her."

"I just want to see if she can move it." Tim turned to Charity, "It's okay, Sweetie, Daddy won't touch it anymore."

"I think it's broken," I said. "We better take her down to Emergency."

"It can't be! She just fell off a chair for Pete's sake," Tim argued.

Tim's family crowded around offering consolation to Charity, but left Tim and me to discuss what should be done. "I think you're overreacting," Tim said. "Look, the floor is carpeted. She maybe fell one foot."

"How did it happen anyway?" I glanced at Tim accusingly, then turned to Charity as she cried. I felt guilty for even thinking it, but the thought kept pressing me, *Why couldn't he watch her closer than that?*

Tim wearily defended himself. "She was sitting on the chair and she kind of stood up to turn around and then flipped right over the side of the wooden arm there."

"That's more than a foot if you ask me," I retorted. "I think we should take her down for an X-ray."

Tim's family was subdued. Tim and I had been married quite young. We had grown up together, bypassing some of the adjustments necessary for two more independent adults marrying. We didn't often argue. Tim's family knew that and seemed uncomfortable hearing us bickering.

"Penny, let's just wait awhile. Maybe she's just overtired. She missed her nap today, you know."

"Okay. We'll wait, but if she's still crying in a half hour I'm taking her down—whether you come or not."

Tim had heard my barbed comment. "Of course, I'll come, too, Penny. I love her, too, you know. I didn't mean for this to happen."

I put my face down in Charity's soft brown hair. "I know, Tim. I know, and I'm sorry for being sharp with you. It's not your fault."

Tim put his arm around me. "I'm sorry she's hurt," he said quietly. "Look, she's sleeping, Pen. Maybe she'll be okay."

We all watched Charity. When she was sleeping soundly, Tim laid her gently on the small couch in the corner of the family room.

Each time she tossed in her sleep she would cry, "Owie! Awwwwh!"

Tim finally said, "We better take her down. She's crying every time she even touches that arm. I can't believe it."

Tim and I took Charity to the Emergency room. In the elevator, I said, "I'm glad it happened here at least. What will we say when we get down there? 'Our son is upstairs in the Burn Center. This is our daughter. She just broke her arm falling off a chair in the waiting room.' "

In spite of everything, Tim laughed. "It's almost funny isn't it." There had been little to laugh about in the past six weeks. Even now, our laughter was occasioned by trauma.

Almost immediately our fears were confirmed. Charity had a fracture in her left arm and another minor crack near it. Her arm in a half-cast and a sling, we returned to the family room. A nurse from the Burn Center met us. "I don't believe it. They called up from emergency and told us what happened. You guys aren't real lucky are you."

The next day our family's medical history was the talk of the Center. What a claim to fame.

I straightened my back, rubbing it briskly with the palm of my hand. It seemed hours since I had put Jeremy on his trike encouraging him to ride around the circular nurses station.

Jeremy's "Eeeeeh" as he cried out in pain stopped me from pushing him too hard. However, we had been told that we had to get him on his feet and soon.

Jeremy was feeling better since he'd been re-grafted. As soon as he was out of the elastomers that restrained him from movement he began to scoot on his bottom all over the Center. He was especially curious about the small wing off the circular station where the very critical patients were kept.

Jeremy voluntarily pushed the pedals on his tricycle only when we would round the circle coming close to the forbidden rooms. Each time we neared the isolated ward, I'd grab the handlebars, for Jeremy was determined to explore that one unknown area of the Burn Center.

"How's he doing?" Marie asked.

"I just can't keep his feet on the pedals—unless we're close to there." I nodded toward the critical care ward. "Will he ever bend that knee again, Marie?" I asked, discouragement filling my voice.

"We'll just have to keep working on it. He walked a couple of steps for me at breakfast."

"Patience has never been my strong suit," I admitted. "It just seems you shouldn't have to teach a kid how to walk more than once in his life."

"Jeremy hasn't been using those leg muscles for a long time, Penny. It's bound to take time to build them up again. Usually the kids do so well. But then if Jeremy's grafts had taken the first time he probably would've too," she mused.

"I'm just glad that's behind us now. Isn't it strange how sick he was last time he was grafted and how well he looks now?"

The next day Tim and I went together to the Center.

Bribing Jeremy with fruit and candy, Tim encouraged him to walk just two steps. His eyes begged for help, but still he staggered toward us, leaning heavily on his left leg and crying, "Eeeeh! Eeeeh!"

Deb and Mike, the couple burned in a car crash, hobbled past cheering Jeremy on. "Did Marie tell you what Jeremy did this morning?" Debbie asked.

"No," Tim said, "What did he do?"

"Marie was sitting in our room visiting with Jeremy in her lap. All of a sudden he got up from her lap and walked five steps over to the M & M jar. You better believe we filled his hands full."

"See, Punky! You can do it!" I cried joyfully.

That afternoon, before we left the Burn Center, I told one of the younger nurses when to expect us back later that evening. In the meantime we were returning home to spend some time with Charity. Auntie Marilyn had returned to Canada with her parents, so Charity was either in the family room with one of us, or staying with various friends. That night we decided to eat supper together at home, something we hadn't done in weeks. Our good friends, Marie and John Peterson, would keep Charity while we visited Jeremy later. We left the Burn Center with the words, "If you need us, call. We can be here in fifteen minutes."

Arriving home I pulled a casserole from the fridge. "Mmmm. This spinach kiesh looks good. Who brought it, Tim?"

"Bev Collova, from Sunday school, dropped it off this morning. She said to pop it in the oven for thirty minutes and it would be ready to eat."

"Penny, why don't you ask Bev for this recipe. It's great," Tim said later as we ate.

"I like it too, Mommy. Can I have more?"

"Sure can, Sweetie." I turned to Tim. "This is really nice. It almost seems like we're a normal family sitting eating here together." I paused. "Especially if Punky were with us too."

Tim and I returned to the hospital that evening with high spirits. At last our son seemed to be improving. When we walked through the big orange doors to the Burn Center, however, something seemed wrong. I gowned quickly and walked into his room. "Where's Jeremy?" I asked John, Jeremy's teenage roommate.

"They moved him, Penny. He was just crying and they moved him." John looked out for Jeremy with a maturity that belied his sixteen young years.

"What happened, John? Why was he crying?"

"That young nurse—she doesn't know him very well. I tried to tell her." John seemed close to tears. "She wouldn't listen to me!"

"John, tell me what happened."

"Jeremy was crying just a little while. I think he was itchy. Anyway, she came in and yelled, 'Stop it right now!' I think Jeremy got real scared and then he really started to cry and fuss. He tried to get out of his bed. She got mad at him. Then they moved him. I told them to leave him alone. That he'd be okay, if she'd leave him alone."

"Thanks, John. I know you did everything you could. Do you know where he is now?"

"I think he's across the circle."

Tim, after parking the car, arrived to hear almost all of our conversation. "I'll go find him," he declared.

Jeremy was tied to the bed. His breath came in short gasps as he cried, "EEEH! EEEH! EEEH! EEEH!" His eyes, red and swollen, were filled with panic. Reaching his restrained hand as close as he could to Tim he pleaded silently to be released. Tim said, "I'll go ask a nurse if it's okay with them."

"I could care less if it's okay!" I spat. "I'm untying him! Why don't you find out what in the world's been going on here."

Tim returned quickly. "Here, Hon, I'll put him in your lap and you can rock him. He isn't here to stay. She said she just put him in here to calm him down."

"How could they do this, Tim?"

"It was the young nurse, she was in charge of Jeremy tonight, and she didn't know how to handle it when he started to cry hard. I think they feel bad about it."

"Why didn't they call us? The last thing I said was to call if they needed us."

Tim stroked Punky's forehead. "It's okay, Punky. Daddy's here. It's okay."

Jeremy's sobbing was silent now. Occasionally his body would jerk involuntarily, but he seemed to relax knowing we were there.

We moved him back to his room and held him until he fell asleep. Just before we left, I spoke to the older charge nurse. "I know this wasn't your fault. You've been very good to Jeremy. But, if this ever happens again, please call us. Restraining Jeremy could really frighten him and maybe even harm him emotionally." A tear slipped down my cheek. "He doesn't understand what we want him to do. It's not that he's being naughty."

The charge nurse nodded. "I know. I'm sorry about what happened. I promise if he gets really upset again we'll call you."

"Even if it's the middle of the night," I said.

"Even if it's the middle of the night," she agreed.

Jeremy began improving. He no longer ran a fever. He was eating well enough that the "nose hose" had been removed. But he was also less able to focus on what was going on around him. We queried the Burn Center staff about the various drugs he'd been on, remembering the resident doctor's suggestion that one of those drugs might be responsible for Jeremy's improved "awareness." Although medications were used to help stem the itching in his healing legs, he now received pain relievers only at bath time. The doctors explained which drugs we could safely try when we got home with Jeremy. We determined to use one at a time, hoping we'd find something to bring back the "old Jeremy" again.

Jeremy seemed different to us than before his burn accident. Even after his regression he had been a happy, trusting child. Now, he seemed easily frustrated, frightened, and spiritless. Jeremy's innocent trust of us as his parents had warmed me on the bleakest of days during his regression. Now he seemed terrified that we too might cause him pain.

Carole, Jeremy's tutor, began coming to the Burn Center twice a week to work with him. Our dear Henry, from the Mounds View School District, had made emergency financial arrangements when he discovered we were paying Carole to tutor Jeremy. Thanks to Henry the school agreed to pay for tutoring until the school year ended.

Previously, Carole had done most of her tutoring carrying Jeremy on her back. Her goal was to encourage the most primitive of communication. She taught Jeremy to slap her hand if he wanted her to go. She sang to him and was rewarded as he repeated phrases or sometimes just sang the tune of a song back to her. After being burned, Jeremy never sang again. Never again did we hear, "Jesus loves me this I know . . ." It was one of our greatest heartaches.

Jeremy's legs were healing, however, and for that we rejoiced. As they healed the itching became unbearable. Medication dulled the irritation, but never seemed able to control it completely, especially as the days wore on.

Often, when Jeremy would cry and cry, insistently slapping his itchy legs, I would ask a nurse, "Is it time yet? Can he have his medication?"

It soon became obvious that the medication was helping very little. Psychologists had visited all of Jeremy's roommates teaching stress reduction strategies and breathing exercises to help them cope with their itching. Because of Jeremy's handicap this kind of therapy was of no use to him.

There were times when Jeremy seemed more playful. One such night, Tim and I had already gone home. Jeremy's legs had been regauzed and ace bandaged. The lights were out and he and his roommates were settled down for the night.

Jeremy's roommate, Fred, whose bed was next to Jeremy's, was a kindly middle-aged man who had a severe alcohol problem. Fred continually called Jeremy, "Jamie" although he was repeatedly corrected.

"Oh, that's right it's Jeremy," he would say. But a few minutes later he would forget.

Fred rang for a nurse shortly after the lights were out.

"Yes, Fred. What is it?" a voice answered from the nurses station.

"I hear noises under my bed. Somebody's . . . under my bed," he insisted in his befuddled sort of way.

"It's probably just the water swishing in your water bed, Fred. Try and go to sleep now," the voice assured.

A few minutes later Fred's light was on again. "Yes, Fred, What is it?" the nurse had responded somewhat impatiently, knowing Fred's thinking wasn't clear anymore.

"I hear something under my bed! I think it's Jamie!"

"I'm sure Jeremy is in his own bed. He can't even walk, and besides, I put the guard rails up." Deciding to humor him however, she reluctantly agreed, "What the heck. I'll come in and check."

The nurse walked in to see a big smile on Jeremy's face. "EEEEEHHH!" he squealed in welcome. He was sitting under Fred's bed.

The next day the doctors said Jeremy could be discharged— *real soon.* Dr. Ahrenholz finalized plans that afternoon. "The day after tomorrow you can take Jeremy home. Therapy must continue, however. Set up a time with Liz, our therapist, to bring him here for daily therapy. She'll also give you a program to follow at home."

"What about the open spot on his left leg?" I asked. "I just can't get him to bend it."

Dr. Ahrenholz' eyes twinkled. "I'm sure you'll figure out ways to work with him at home. I heard at staffing today that you've been taping Jeremy's feet to the trike to get his knee to bend."

Laughing, I replied, "I was hoping you wouldn't find out about that. I want you to know I did clear it with a nurse first."

The following day Tim came and watched the nurses bathe Jeremy. The next day we both were required to do Jeremy's bath, apply the moisturizing cream, treat the open spots, bandage and ace wrap his legs and torso. Even the donor sites needed to be double ace wrapped for several months to prevent scar tissue from growing thick. We learned the bandaging needed to be done with a certain twist of the wrist. It had to be firm but not tight enough to stop the circulation. Jeremy was a nonverbal child who wouldn't be able to tell us if he was having pain or loss of feeling because we'd bandaged him too tightly. So this step was of particular concern.

Neither Tim nor I had seen Jeremy's legs since we saw them coated with clear greenish plastic at the fire. We had heard many times from staff in the Burn Center, "His legs looked great today." We would stare at his legs, scrawny even with thick gauze bandages and two layers of ace wrappings, and think, *Beautiful? Well, maybe. . . .*

I got special permission to enter the Burn Center early and sit with Jeremy until his turn for a bath. Jeremy's roommate, John, was also ready to leave the Center. Staples held many of his special dressings in place on his back donor sites. I could hear him screaming as they removed each one. My stomach churned. Maybe they're were right not to let families in here at bath time.

Tim came in, breathless, after seeing the daycare center children off to school and arranging for the substitute to feed the kindergartners lunch at Kids' Kottage.

"We're next Tim. I'm afraid I'll be sick. One of the mothers fainted last week when she saw the bath."

"I didn't think it was too bad yesterday, Hon. You'll do fine. I'll do the main part since I've seen them do it already."

We walked into the steamy room. The two large tubs, separated with moveable curtains, looked out of place in the large, sparsely furnished room.

Tim and I carefully unwrapped Jeremy's legs. He lifted them each in turn, already familiar with the routine. As we unwrapped the last layer of gauze bandages I struggled to keep my composure. His skin was a deep uneven red. At some points, I could see a diamond pattern on his legs where I knew skin had been grafted. Several holes exposed yellowish flesh deep inside. Uneven skin clung to his bones. His knees looked like huge knobs linked by skinny sticks. More uniform in color and texture than his legs, Jeremy's back and torso had deep, red stripes where his donor skin had been shaved.

Claudia seemed to sense my shock. "His legs won't look so red as the months go on. They'll get to be a more normal looking color eventually."

"I didn't think it would be this bad." I turned away briefly, drawing a deep breath. "They were so beautiful." Tears filled my eyes.

Jeremy cried loudly, "EEEEEHH! EEEEEEH!" the entire time he was in the bath. Flailing blindly, he shoved Tim's hands away from the deep open wounds Tim scrubbed with sterile gauze.

"That's good, Tim," Candy, the head nurse of the Burn Center, encouraged. "You need to get them clean or we'll get infection in there. I know it's hard to do, but you just have to get in there and clean the open areas well."

As soon as we lifted Jeremy from the water he stopped screaming as if on cue. We finished the bandaging with sweat running down our faces, and it wasn't only because it was hot in the bath room.

Candy congratulated us. "You did it. You'll do just fine at home, I know. Jeremy's lucky to have parents like you two."

I looked at Candy, her long blonde hair caught up in a bun. She was a large, but beautiful woman with a great sense of humor. I suspected she had much to do with the cooperative spirit among the staff in the Center. "Candy, I don't know how we would've gotten through this time without all of you to help us."

Tim and I packed up Jeremy's toys and belongings while Jeremy was passed from nurse to nurse for final hugs and goodbyes. Five huge red plastic bags stood at the door full of gifts and cards sent from all over the world. Nearby, sat Jeremy's trike, ready to be used in therapy at home. When at last the car was packed and Jeremy sat snugly in my lap, his legs elevated with a pillow, Tim started the engine of our red Opel and said, "Here we go Punky Boy! We're going home at last!"

15

"Mommy, I Stepped on God!"

In the weeks following Jeremy's arrival home, our lives were controlled by his burn injury. Although Jeremy had learned to walk again by leaning heavily on his left leg, he would crumple at our feet after just a few yards, crying to be carried.

Tim and I traded off taking Punky to physical therapy. At first we took him every day, but when his right leg regained some mobility we needed to take him only three times a week. The underpart of his right knee remained our biggest concern. He was burned deeply there. The graft had never taken or filled in even though we continued to bathe him twice a day, putting special antibiotic cream on it to prevent infection. Each time the area began to heal the flesh would burst open again. Jeremy's baths continued to be excruciating because the wound was so deep and exposed.

The physical stress of carrying Punky, now five years old, bathing him amid screams of agony, administering meds in an effort to control his itching, gauzing, and ace bandaging his legs as well as bracing the one to straighten it, teaching at Kids' Kottage Daycare Center, and making the repeated trips for physical therapy, was taking a toll on all of us.

Charity, normally an easy going child, had insisted on sleeping in our bed since coming home from Grandma's. Otherwise she remained loveable and easy to handle so we were not fully aware of the stress she was feeling.

One day, shortly after Jeremy had come home from the hospital, we sent the Kids' Kottage children off to school, and prepared the bandages and creams for Jeremy's morning bath. Tim and I unwrapped his ace and gauze bandages carefully and then set him gingerly in the lukewarm bath. Jeremy began to scream pathetically in a high pitched EEEEEEHHHHHHH sound.

My stomach churned as I forced myself to scrub the vulnerable yellowish flesh exposed by his open wounds. I was getting used to the sight of his skinny fat-less legs now, but still when the bandages came off for bath time their unevenness and red color would shock me again. Tim and I were almost finished when I realized Jeremy's screaming was matched by a smaller voice in our bedroom. Curious, I hurried in there. Charity was running in front of the mirrored wall, fists clenched, tears chasing down her cheeks, crying, "Stop it! Stop it, Mommy and Daddy! Leave my brother alone!"

"Honey, What's the matter?" I asked gently.

"Mommy, he doesn't want a bath. I hate it when he screams!" Pausing for breath she finally blurted, "Why can't you and Daddy leave my brother alone?"

"Chari, we have to bathe him. It's hard for Daddy and Mommy too, but if we don't Jeremy will get infection and have to go back to the Burn Center."

I hugged her tiny figure close to me hoping she would at least feel the security of my love.

One day about six weeks after Jeremy left the hospital, a burn checkup was scheduled along with his routine physical therapy. I was relieved that it was Tim's turn to take him.

Jeremy's autism made it difficult for him to be in crowds. The long waits in the Burn Center waiting room were often unbearable. We tried food, songs, books, and walks to pass what seemed like an interminable amount of time, but Jeremy's short attention span discouraged even our most creative efforts. When waits for burn checks stretched to an hour or two a lot of songs, walks, apples, and patience were used up.

While waiting for Tim and Jeremy to return from the Burn Center, I stirred up a batch of caramel rolls. Soon the smell of sweet bread dough filled the kitchen as I punched and turned the mixture until it was smooth and elastic. Spreading the caramel-colored sugar mixed with cinnamon on the buttered dough, I hoped the fresh caramel rolls would brighten the day for Charity and me, and be a pleasant surprise for Tim and Jeremy when they returned home from the Burn Center.

Charity sped past me on her tricycle in the daycare center kitchen as I scrubbed the sticky caramel roll dough off the orange countertop. Her shoulder length hair flew as she drove around the tables into the game room and back. The caramel rolls, now baking in the oven, smelled of cinnamon and carmel, reminding me of my own mother's kitchen.

Baking was always a special time for my mother, sisters, and me. It was one of the times we would really talk. Indeed, it was happy childhood memories that induced me to continue making homemade bread, if for nothing more than to remind me of my roots.

The oven timer rang. With mitted hands, I pulled out the pans of golden rolls from the racks. *Oooh, that's hot!* I thought, tipping the pans to release the rolls. Charity came whizzing by singing, "I don't like Goawwed! I don't like Gooawed!"

What is she singing? I thought, this time listening carefully to her sing-song. Again I heard, "I don't like Goawwed! I don't like Goawwed!" as her trike whizzed past me into the game room.

Charity rounded the corner coming toward me.

I stopped her trike and knelt in front of her. "Charity, what are you singing?"

"I'm singing, 'I don't like God!' " she stated matter-of-factly.

Trying not to show my distress, I queried, "Chari, why don't you like God? He loves you."

"Mommy," she responded somewhat impatiently, "God doesn't like me. So I don't like him; He's naughty to you and Tim." Charity mimicked the older children in our center, who called us by our first names.

"Chari, God likes you. He loves you."

"Oh no, He doesn't!" Charity said sticking her chin out firmly.

I sighed and tried another approach. "What makes you think God doesn't like you?"

"He's mad to me."

"Why do you feel God is mad at you?"

Charity's brown eyes were tremulous as she whispered, "Be . . . be . . . cause I stepped on Him."

I picked my little girl up, sat her on the kitchen counter, and said, "Charity, why do you think you stepped on God?"

"Well, you said God was 'divisible, I didn't know where He was, so I think I stepped on Him and then He got mad to me and—" She stopped and looked at me as if to see if I were trustworthy of her deepest secret.

"What, Honey?"

"And that's why Jerem' got burned. That's why God's naughty

to you and Tim." With a deep breath she finished, "And that's why I don't like God."

Finally, understanding the pain and responsibility she was feeling, I rushed to explain. "God loves you. He's not mad at you."

Charity interrupted. "Well, it hurts a lot when you get stepped on."

"Chari, you didn't step on God."

"Well, then why is he naughty to you and Tim?"

"God didn't make Jeremy get burned. He was just burned because he happened to hit the switch on the stove and he was wearing pants that burned super fast."

Realizing she still didn't understand I decided to give myself some time to answer, on a two-and-a-half-year-old's level, the universal problem of pain. In the tradition of my childhood, I began our first mother-daughter talk while baking. "Look, Char', let's have a mommy-girl talk. You help me and we'll have a little coffee party with caramel rolls. Okay?"

As we sat sipping our coffee (mine was black, Charity's was white with two tablespoons of coffee), I said, "Now, listen real carefully. This is a story of how the whole world began. When I'm all through we'll see if you understand why Jeremy got burned. Okay?"

Charity nodded.

"It all started with Adam and Eve. Remember the Creation story on your tape?"

"You mean the "Bare-naked-Adam tape?"

"Yes," I laughed. "That's the one."

Continuing, I explained, "God made man because He was so lonely and He wanted friends. God had angels in heaven, but they were without a free will, which means they couldn't decide if they loved God or not. They had to do what they were supposed to.

"God thought, 'I'll make man and woman so they can choose to love each other and love Me or, they can choose not to . . . .' "

I searched Charity's face to see if she was with me, before I continued. "God made the first choice to be about eating from a tree of knowledge. God said, 'If you eat of this tree you shall die.' What happened, Char?"

"They ate from that tree."

"That's right, they chose to disobey God. And when they did, death became part of the world. That meant for the first time people would get sick, be hungry, have rough times, and die."

"Mommy, why does that make Jeremy burned?"

"It's because, Chari, when sin and death came into the world our great, great, great, great grandmas and grandpas, anyway people a long time ago, kept making choices. Some were good and some were bad. All of those choices affected the lives of other people, those around them and those still to be born. God must have felt sad when He saw some of the bad choices people made. Things like killing other people. But He had made a promise to give man and woman free choice and God doesn't go back on His promises. Do you think God wants people to kill little babies, Chari?"

"No. Why would He?"

"We know little babies get killed sometimes, don't we?"

"Yeah, is God mad to them, too?"

"No, Honey. That's the whole point of the story. God gave man choice and He won't take the choice away by stopping even bad things from happening."

Slipping into our personal names again, she said, "Penny, I thought you and Tim said God can do anything?"

"God can. But God doesn't go back on his promises even when it must be hard not to. Do you think God wanted Jeremy to be burned?"

"No, but Mommy, don't you think I could've stepped on God since He's 'divisible'?"

"No, because God is a spirit. When he sent Jesus, He had a body, but in heaven and on earth God doesn't need one so no matter where you walk you'll never step on God."

"So, God's not mad to me, huh?"

"No, Charity, God is not mad to you and He's not naughty to Daddy and me, either. It's just the way life is, that hard things sometimes happen. You want to know one good part, though?"

"Is it short?" Charity was getting a little impatient by now. I wasn't surprised, although I continued to be amazed at her incredible verbal and receptive skills.

"Sure. See God knew that death and bad stuff were in the world so He sent His Son Jesus to die for all of His friends so we can go to heaven when we die. In heaven do you think Jeremy will be autistic?"

"I don't know."

"Nope, he won't be. He'll talk and sing again and he won't even have scars anymore." My voice broke.

"Not even baths anymore?"

"No, Hon, that's the good part. There's one more thing. No matter how much bad stuff happens to us while we live here guess who promised never to leave us?"

"God?"

"Yeah. Does God keep His promises?"

"Mommy!" Charity said in exasperation, "That's what you just said! Now, if you're done can I have another caramel roll?"

16

When a Child Suffers

The farmyards crusted with frost looked like still life paintings as Tim and I sped on our way to Oak Hills Bible College in the early morning hours. Bemidji, in northern Minnesota, was still freezing cold, even though it was late March. Oak Hills' memories reminded me that in Bemidji spring yielded it's budding trees and flowers only reluctantly, even in May. Today, the cold clear air seemed definitely of a winter vintage. We drove in silence enjoying the grand display of nature.

Finally, Tim spoke, "Penny, I know how painful the memories of the fire are for both of us, but we can't wait any longer. Why don't you start reading to me your notes. I'll try to fill in with my recollections. From that, we should be able to complete the outline of what we'll share today."

Tim was referring to the Oak Hills Alumni Conference. Candie Blankman, my former college roommate, had asked us to speak at a seminar on, "When a Child Suffers." Only four months had passed since Jeremy's burn accident. Although Tim and I were reluctant to open the scabs on our wounds, we both believed the exercise would further hone our personal belief system as well as allow us to communicate to others with greater clarity, regarding suffering and the sovereignty of God.

Individually, we had prepared for the seminar by reading several books and articles on suffering, as well as by gathering material we had studied earlier in our lives. What Tim and I hadn't been able to talk about yet was the fire.

As we drove the one hundred and fifteen miles from my parents' farm, where we had left Jeremy and Charity, to Oak Hills, we reminisced about the events surrounding Jeremy's burn injury.

When we turned down Oak Hills Road our thoughts returned to happier times. I pointed excitedly down a narrow winding lane.

"Look, there's the trailer I lived in my second year at Oak Hills." I strained to see through the rear window the tiny trailer nestled in the Norway pines. "Remember when you'd come from Winnipeg to visit me my second year? I'd bake you a cherry pie in that little kitchen."

Tim laughed. "And sometimes it would be gone before I got there if word got out on campus you were baking pies."

I put my hand on Tim's knee. "Yeah, those were the days. We were so happy, so carefree. I guess I thought our life together would always be like that."

"Guess I did too, Hon, although Mr. T. did push us to think beyond our naivete. He was the first person to challenge me to demand that what I believed about God should be logical; that I should seek truth and in doing that I would find God—who is truth."

"Yeah, Tim, I'm really thankful we had Mr. T.'s teaching to fall back on with all we've been through. At least we had some place to start when we began searching to understand God's role in suffering."

"That's right," Tim echoed as we pulled into the parking lot beside the Administration Building.

A short while later we walked to the chapel where we were to present our seminar. Fond memories flooded over me as I looked around the simple auditorium. I could almost hear the harmony of Thursday chapel hymn sings. I captured again the sweet fellowship of communion services. I smiled remembering the many chapels Tim and I sat through holding hands beneath our Bibles.

"Penny! Tim!" Candie squealed, interrupting my reverie. "I've been looking all over for you two."

"We just got here," Tim said, his eyes twinkling as he watched Candie and me hug each other, joyfully prancing around the room.

"How's my favorite roommate?" she asked.

"We're doing okay, Candie. This is going to be a heavy one," I said, serious now.

"I know." Her eyes filled with tears. "Are you sure you'll be okay? This is all still so fresh for you. In fact, when I asked you to come, I wouldn't have been surprised if you'd turned me down."

"We'll be all right," Tim assured. "I just hope that what we have to share will help someone else."

Our conversation was cut short as people began moving into the auditorium. Among our audience were our dear friends, Gary and Cheryl, parents themselves now of a handicapped child. Vicki, a newer friend, was the mother of Ginger, an eight-year-old girl, who was diagnosed with leukemia around the time of Jeremy's accident.

We began by recreating that painful Sunday, November 21, 1982, when Tim saw Jeremy at the door of the daycare center in flames.

I told the story of our earlier belief in God's protection for Jeremy and our shock, then, when he was burned. I could feel the empathy of the audience. They cringed at the pain Jeremy had endured.

"Our family's experience isn't unique," Tim said. "Many of you have suffered or seen your children suffer. Today, we not only want to share our own experience with suffering, but to challenge you to think about God's role in suffering."

I interjected. "Many people who really tried to help us when Jeremy was burned, were, in effect giving a Bandaid response to a major injury. Well-meaning friends and relatives wanted to find a reason for God allowing this to happen. However, our situation made some uncomfortable. If they accepted that Jeremy was burned just because he climbed on top of a stove and knocked a burner switch on, then they would also have to concede that something bad could happen to them or to their family, over which they had no control.

"Many believe that if they pray for protection for their children, their kids will then always have a full stomach, never be killed in a traffic accident, or be burned in a fire. We had this mistaken belief, too.

"Our belief that God would bless our family with protection crumbled at our feet when we stood in the Burn Center on that Sunday afternoon, even though that very day we had prayed for God's protection for Jeremy. When we saw our Punky, who couldn't even so much as cry, 'It hurts, Mommy and Daddy! It hurts!' hooked up to machines and fighting for his life, when we saw Jeremy's beautiful legs become, in a matter of minutes, scrawny sticks wrapped in thick bandages and oozing with blood, we knew what we'd been believing wasn't making sense."

I nodded to Tim to take over for awhile. He swallowed hard and then began. "Penny and I have compiled a list of explanations we were given for Jeremy's regression and burn accident.

"Some told us that Jeremy was suffering 'so we would grow spiritually.' We received a card with this quote, 'What we call adversity, God calls opportunity; what we call tribulation, God calls growth.' We were forced to ask the question: Must God burn children to affect their parent's spiritual growth?

"Another reason we heard was that it happened 'for your good and God's glory.' This seemed ludicrous. When we bathe Jeremy twice a day and listen to him scream as we scrub his vulnerable open areas, we sense only a fraction of the pain he endured the six weeks he was without skin. Are we so intent on being considered 'spiritual' that we could be sadistic enough to say, 'Yes, it's good Jeremy is screaming in pain. It's for our good.' We know it isn't for his good.

"We were further told that Jeremy was burned 'to make our values more Christ-like.' We have seen that this is often a result of suffering, reminding us that God and people are more important than success and things. But is it logical to assume that God specifically chose a child to suffer because of the imperfect values of his parent? I think not.

"Several gave the reason 'so that others will believe in God.' This answer seems the greatest paradox to us." Tim smiled wryly. "Often people are agnostics because they can't believe in a God who would allow the suffering and starvation they see in the world around them.

" 'To bring community and love among believers' was another possible reason given to us. This reminds me of a pastor whose teenage daughter's leg was amputated as a result of cancer. The church had been having political wars for sometime, but as a result of the accident declared a truce. The pastor was told, 'You see this is why Becky lost her leg. This church is pulling together like never before.' He responded, 'What will it take next time to stop your fighting, her other leg? Her arms? Her life?'

"It was additionally suggested that the tragedy happened so 'we would know how to help others who suffer.' The Bible does tell us we will be able to comfort others as a result of our suffering. We have seen that happen many times in our own lives. However, as an intrinsic reason for human suffering, it does not hold up. If there were no suffering, no comforters would be needed.

"We were frequently reminded 'God must especially love you for He chastens those he loves.' We do experience some kinds of suffering as a result of our own fallen choices. But human suffering seems to result from the general fallen nature of the world.

"Another rationale we were given was this: 'Handicapped children are sent by God to specially chosen parents.' For a long time we believed this to be true. Then we learned that the divorce rate among parents of handicapped children or of a child who has died is very high. The child abuse rate for handicapped children is also incredibly high. Although Penny and I try to be good parents to Jeremy, we have to ask, 'Does God love Jeremy more than the handicapped children who have been locked in closets, placed in institutions from birth, or burned with cigarette butts?' Why didn't God send them to the home of 'special parents'?"

I let out a low whistle. "That's quite a list isn't it? Many of you may now be saying, 'Don't you think there is a purpose, any purpose, for Jeremy to suffer?'"

A hand shot up in the back of the room. "What about miracles?" I smiled back, "Yes, what about miracles? Let's first look at what Scripture says in Romans 8:28. We'll then explain what we've come to believe about the sovereignty of God as it relates to suffering and I'll include a brief statement about miracles at that point. Okay?" He nodded.

"I'll read the verse in the King James Version. 'And we know that all things work together for good to them that love God, to them who are the called according to his purpose.' This verse may very well be the most often quoted verse in relation to suffering.

"It's meaning is often assumed to be, 'all things work together for good, therefore our sovereign God causes all things to happen.' This is not necessarily an illogical assumption from this translation. I'll come back to this verse in a moment.

"The first problem comes when we look for support for this interpretation in the rest of Scripture. The second when we acknowledge all the pain and evil in the world around us. Could God really be just and cause the annihilation of six million Jews in the Holocaust? Could God really be merciful and allow rapists to go scot free while their victims suffer irreparably? Is it God's plan for thousands of African parents to watch helplessly as their children starve to death?

"Mr. T. made this observation when we were students here at Oak Hills. 'One of the outstanding attributes of God is His sorrow at the suffering of humankind. There is nothing to be sorry about if things are the way He wants them to be.'

"In an article 'Suffering Must Have Meaning,' Jon Tal

Murphree writes about twelve missionary familiy members who were brutally hacked to death by terrorist guerrillas in Zimbabwe.

> *I am appalled at the way God is so often blamed for the wicked terrifying atrocities of evil men! Can anyone really believe that God put those killers up to that barbaric crime? Why should the blame for the brutal acts of madmen be pinned on God. Someone argues, "But God is supposed to be in charge of everything," Then my response is, "How so, and who said?" This would make robots out of people and leave them with no freedom at all.**

"This is not to assume that it is safe to base our theology solely on life experience. However, when our theology doesn't match with the reality we see in the world around us, we need to ask, not 'Is the Bible wrong?' but instead, 'Have we been interpreting the Bible correctly?' "

I paused, giving our listeners a chance to digest what I was saying. "What of Romans 8:28 then? The *New International Version* translates it this way: 'And we know that in all things God works for the good of those who love him, who have been called according to his purpose.' Why does this translation seem more logical? Because Scripture as a whole says nothing about all things 'working together for good.'

"Even though God is able to bring good out of evil situations, it does not follow that he intended or caused rape, murder, poisonous pollution, child abuse, and other bad things. God's power to bring good out of evil, doesn't make the evil good."

Tim spoke again. "God is not the author of sin or the results of our fallenness. God made the world system for the overall purpose of having humans do good because they choose to do so.

"The potential for choosing good was given first to Adam and Eve, but they chose otherwise.

"As their descendants, we are corporately part of this fallen world, members of a fallen race. Corporately, we face the disease, death, and evil which is a byproduct of sin's influence through the ages. Individually, we are guilty of our own sin and are recipients of the results of our own choices as well as the choices of others. The choices of all humans since the fall in Eden have affected not only the individual 'choosers' but the people around

*Quoted in Asbury College *Ambassador* (Spring 1978).

them and the generations that followed them."

Tim then summarized by reading from our annual family Christmas letter.

> *We have come to believe that in God's gift of a free will, by which we became humans instead of robots, good and evil co-exist. With this disease, death, and famine became part of our world scene. We have experienced some of the ashes of the fallen world these past two years. In all we have seen there is nothing happening, as a result of the fallen world, that God in His sovereignty cannot help us cope with, or no situation in which He will leave us alone.*

"I think I understand what you mean," said the man who had spoken earlier, "but I still want to know how this relates to Jesus' miracles of healing?"

"Aha. Finally, we get to your earlier question," I replied.

"It deserves more time than we have right now, however, I'd like to make this comment. Miracles in the New Testament appeared to happen to show God to be God. Even then people were poverty stricken, sick, and dying. God's purpose in miracles didn't seem to be then or now to provide believers with a 'cushy' existence.

"That miracles are possible is obvious. We do not live in a closed system where God cannot intervene. God is God after all! The question is this: Will God routinely intervene in a way that sets aside the way His world usually runs? When I look at the world around me, it appears to me that God's great miracle is that we are indeed human, that our choices are indeed freely made, and that in spite of the dung of the fallen world, flowers still bud, birds still sing, people still love. If that's not a miracle, then what is?"

Glancing at the clock in the back of the chapel, Tim said, "Penny, can you tie all of this together before we have a question time?"

My throat was suddenly dry. I was amazed at the level of concentration I read on the faces of those before us. This was heavy stuff.

"When Tim and I realized that God wasn't pulling strings to allow suffering in the life of Jeremy, specifically, we were freed to really love God. Suffering is a result of the world we live in. God isn't doing it.

"Suddenly we realized, if God were intervening and interfering with the choices of men and women and the natural flow of the world, He would be denying the humanness He Himself created.

"We know that many of you here today are hurting. For others of you, life is going along right according to schedule. You may think, 'This isn't relevant for me.' To you, I offer a challenge: suffering is part of earth-side living. The suffering are not specially chosen out by God to suffer for a specific reason, anymore than you are especially blessed or privileged by Him. I urge you to wrestle with this issue. When we were students at Oak Hills, Mr. T. challenged us to demand logic from what we believed. We suggest you do the same. Seek truth. It will revolutionize your life. How you pray. How you live. And most particularly, how you comfort the suffering.

"Three questions I'd like to leave you with: First, Is it possible the belief, 'that our trust in God will guarantee us health and prosperity' comes only because we are a comfortable, wealthy nation, with access to money and medicine which most of the rest of the world does not have?

"Second, are we American Christians more deserving of a comfortable life than our Third World brothers and sisters?

"Third, do we want a guarantee of personal protection, good health, and prosperity so badly that we would dare bend our theology to include promises God has never given us?

"These are questions, like the one mentioned earlier about miracles, that deserve much more consideration than we can give them here. Please think about them, especially before giving glib reasons for suffering which are supported neither by Scripture or reality."

When we opened the group to discussion we were amazed at the degree of honesty and openness with which individuals shared. Finally Tim said, "We really have to close. I want you to know how much Penny and I have appreciated your willingness to hear our story and what we now believe about suffering."

As we prepared to leave, an older woman marched up to me. "I want you to know, I think you are dead wrong." Her jaw was set firmly as she continued stoutly, "I'm going to pray for you."

"Great we can use your prayers," I said. "We've just shared what we believe to be true from our experiences and study. You're free to believe what you choose."

I turned to where Candie and Tim stood waiting. The woman grabbed my arm. "I'll tell you why you're wrong. My nephew, he got married. He wasn't a believer and wouldn't go to church.

Then a couple of years later he got divorced. After the divorce he became a Christian . . . so you see," she finished triumphantly.

"See what?" I answered feebly.

"God caused the divorce because he knew it was the only way he'd make my nephew a Christian."

I swallowed hard. "It's wonderful your nephew is reconciled to God. And I agree that it's marvelous God can reach out to us even in the tragedies of life, but I don't agree with you that God caused or planned your nephew's divorce. I would say instead, with Jon Tal Murphree, 'God used what was not His purpose to serve His purpose.' "

It was almost eleven p.m. when we got into our red Opel to return to my parents' home. "Can we call them to let them know we're on the road?" I asked when we were a little ways up the road. "I think they may have expected us sooner than we'll make it now."

"Okay, Penny. I'll pull into this station and you run in and call."

I hurried inside and dialed the number.

"Penny. You aren't on your way yet?" My mother, always in control, was crying.

"No, we're just leaving. What's wrong?"

"Jeremy has been crying and itching so bad some of his grafts are bleeding. We don't know what to do."

"Did you try bathing him?" I asked.

"We did that twice already. Charity is sitting next to me, right now, telling me just how to lotion his legs and how tight to make his aces. I don't know what I'd do if she wasn't here to help. I'm so afraid I'll bandage his legs too tightly."

"She's a good sister."

"She sure is. She holds Jeremy's hands while I lotion him and says, 'It's okay, Punky Boy, Sissy's here.' "

"It sounds as if you're doing all you can, Mom. We'll be there as soon as we can make it."

I hung up the phone with a heavy weight filling my stomach.

Climbing into the car, I said, "Tim, we shouldn't have stayed this long. Jeremy's itching. Mom sounds really upset.

"What are we going to do, Tim? If Mom and Dad can't cope with Jeremy for a day, who can?" My voice broke. "How are we going to make it all alone?"

Tim looked at me, his brown eyes sad. "It's not over yet, is it Honey?"

I shook my head, tears sliding off my cheeks. "Sometimes, I feel like I'll never be happy again, not in that lighthearted kind of way we were in college."

"Our lives aren't the same as they were then, Penny."

We drove in silence for awhile. Then I said, "You know, those nights when Jeremy's so itchy that he's awake all night, and we try to comfort him, and nothing helps?"

"Yeah. How can I forget? It happens almost every other night."

"If I believed God specifically purposed Jeremy's suffering, especially those sleepless nights of endless itching, I couldn't go on."

"I know what you mean," Tim said quietly. "I'm glad we've finally realized God is on our side. If we thought God was doing this to Jeremy for some reason known only to Him—how could we trust Him?"

"I guess that's why sharing today was so meaningful. It seems imperative to me that people know that suffering is a result of a fallen world and that God is on their side."

Tim reached over the black shift stick and squeezed my hand tightly. "God is on our side, too, but I have no delusions that our life is going to be easy."

"I know," I agreed softly.

It was sleeting now. I saw the windshield wipers moving rhythmically back and forth, back and forth. As I watched the arc of the silver blades making their pendulum swing, it seemed as if in cadence, they chanted my thoughts of Jeremy. I saw his skinny, disfigured legs. I watched him run as if trying to escape his own skin from the itching that threatened to control him. I heard his autistic silence. I felt his pain. A pain we share together, for he's our son and we love him.

Epilogue

Pastor Mike Bortel is now the Pastor of Counsel and Care at Faith Covenant Church in Burnsville, Minnesota. Mike recently published *Step Biblically*, the parenting curriculum he developed while teaching our Beta Sunday School Class.

Pastor Hart Christianson suffered a second, fatal heart attack in September, 1985. He is greatly missed by all who loved him.

Al, Jeremy's hospital roommate from North Dakota, has recovered well and resumed farming his family homestead. Al and Madge remain a strong support system to us; they serve as a reminder that God is not limited to one denomination.

Darla and Steve live in rural Minnesota and are proud parents of Grant, now seven, as well as a new baby girl.

My mom and dad still farm in Rose City, Minnesota.

Tim's mom lives near Winnipeg, Manitoba. We were saddened in April of 1986 by the sudden death of Tim's father.

Our Family

Angele made us five in January, 1984 and brought to each of us hope and joy during the valley of our lives.

Charity, now seven, is a sensitive and loving second grader at Island Lake School. She continues to be our family "theologian."

Tim and I still operate Kids' Kottage Daycare Center in Shoreview, Minnesota and continue to be amazed at how much there is to learn when working with children. I am also a part time student finishing a degree in Family Counseling. Tim has nearly completed his building projects at Kids' Kottage and also runs his part time business, Dove Security Systems—a burglar alarm installation company.

The five years following Jeremy's burn accident have passed in a blur of sleepless nights, trial and error medication testing, baths, ace-bandaging, therapy, new teachers, and hiring of respite staff to relieve us so we could keep up with the never-ending routine.

Jeremy's hyperactivity and low functioning ability did not improve with the medication we had hoped would help him after leaving the Burn Center. We lived in fear that he would get hurt again, and so we watched him constantly. Even so, he would occasionally escape our watch and and run away to the neighbors or the nearby Catholic church. Once, shortly after Jeremy had regained full use of his legs, he voluntarily participated in mass. I, not so happily volunteered to retrieve him, hoping against hope I'd get to him before he drank the communion wine or ate a candle. (I didn't wait around to find out.)

Two years ago, Tim took Jeremy to Dr. Backus, his pediatric neurologist, for a checkup. Jeremy was excited about the new environment. In his enthusiasm, he dumped a plant, rearranged the pictures on the walls and examined the doctor. Dr. Backus didn't even try to examine Jeremy, but instead chose to observe him. Finally, he turned to Tim and asked, "Are you and Penny still married?"

Tim nodded affirmatively, at the same time diving for Jeremy who was after the plant again.

"You must be doing something right," he remarked.

Then he added soberly, "Unfortunately, I still have to say there is nothing I can do for Jeremy, so whatever it is you're doing to survive, keep doin' it."

Jeremy, now ten-years-old, attends a special school. We are sure now his autistic-likeness is caused by a neurological problem with a metabolic origin. Medication is controlling newly diagnosed seizure activity and has resulted in fewer "spells" of crying and head banging.

Jeremy is one of the "rare" autistic children who does not seem able to progress. He has probably said less than ten words in the past five years. His ability to communicate is further hampered by the fact that he can't understand language; it's as if he is a stranger in a foreign country. Jeremy's other senses are extraordinarily acute, however. He still loves unique textures and tastes crayons and other non-edibles as often as he gets a chance. His ear for music is incredible as evidenced by loud wailing when he hears imperfect pitch. His coordination is also amazing. His phys-ed teacher said, "If we could just get Jeremy to kick the ball where we want him to he'd be some soccer player."

Jeremy is a great hugger—and sometime kisser. If he graces you by sitting in your lap you know you are on his "very special list."

Although Jeremy hasn't made any great neurological improvements in the five years since he was burned, just two weeks ago he went to the cupboard, took out a cup, turned on the water, and got himself a drink. Charity, Angele, and I gave him a standing ovation. Now, all we have to do is teach him to turn the water off.

The challenge to raise Jeremy in a society that prioritizes things he can't contribute to it, such as money, prestige and power, is at times awesome. Beyond that our family is handicapped in some ways as a result of Jeremy's autism. Eating out, going to the zoo, attending church are not options for us to participate in as a family unit anymore. Also, Jeremy is growing. I can no longer lift him—or outrun him. Even so, I find it easier to cope with his handicap now. This may be because of his new medication, or that we have organized a respite care system, or that Jeremy has finally stopped "itching" from his burns, or that we've just gotten used to "living on the edge."

In any case, our family functions pretty well most of the time. We laugh. We swim and go boating together—activities Jeremy loves. We enjoy special family times such as building a fire and making popcorn as the coals burn down.

We have a small group of intimate friends who love us just as we are . . . and accept and love Jeremy as he is. Marie and John Peterson and their boys, Erik and Jeffrey, continue to enrich our lives. They are indeed "family" to us.

Our friendship with Karen and Mark Baden and their children, Matt and Ali, reached a depth few friendships do after the heartache of the fire drew us together.

The strength of these friendships has enabled us to be strong when our "handicapped" family makes some other acquaintances uncomfortable.

Recently, Tim and I were discussing how Jeremy's suffering has affected our marriage. Although we have great empathy for the many whose marriages have not survived the trauma of their children's suffering, we feel it's important to share the "good" which only God could bring out of the pain of our child's suffering.

Tim made this observation, "You always wonder, 'What will we do if tragedy strikes?' Well, we know. We don't have to wonder anymore."

As a result of Jeremy's handicap we feel less burdened to perform, to be 'the perfect family.' We aren't even in the race.

Jeremy reminds us of our humanity. When we are overwhelmed with love for him, even though he is not the child we had originally dreamed of, we are reminded of God's parental love for us, as we struggle in our handicapped humanity.

The history I share with Tim uniquely bonds us. Who but Tim could understand my pain and loss? Who but Tim could love our autistic son as I?

Because Jeremy's condition forces us to curtail many outside activities, we have more time to "be a family." Often, we sing a little family theme song: *We are a family. Daddy the kids and me. We are a family!* YES WE ARE!

In fact, occasionally in our daily "family living" we forget those earlier days that inspired me to write this book and then something happens to remind us. One of those times of remembrance happened recently.

Tim was registering Charity for a summer school support group for siblings of autistic children in the Autism Program. I was busy at the daycare center while he was away. Tim wasn't gone long, in fact he surprised me when he came home in just over an hour.

"Hi!" I said, not even turning to look from the accounts I was billing, "Didn't expect you home so soon."

"Penny?"

"Yeah, Just a sec,' Honey. I have one statement left." Then looking up, I noticed. Tim was crying. "Tim, what happened?" I reached out to hold him.

"It was kinda hard today," he said. I was signing consent forms in the reception area when a beautiful little girl came in with her mom. She screamed and screamed. Her mom said she probably thought it was a doctor's office."

"How old was she?" I interrupted.

"About five, I think. I think she was there for the diagnostic summer school program. Anyway, pretty soon there were a whole bunch of staff people there."

"Sheila, too?"

"Yeah. And nothing they did calmed her down. I mean, she just didn't understand. Her eyes were filled with terror."

"It got to you, huh?"

Tim nodded. His eyes were red and a tear slipped from his cheek. "I guess I get so used to Jeremy. Seeing him cry in frustration, hearing 'EEEHH!' all day long, that I almost forget what it must be like for him. He must feel just as terrified as that little girl, Penny."

I reached out and took Tim's big hand in mine, waiting for him to continue. Tim smiled wryly, "I thought about that little girl and cried all the way home. Penny, it's a tragedy that the minds of beautiful little kids won't work, that they must live their whole lives in fear and frustration. It's just unbelievable that some people claim God has a reason for things like this to happen. There isn't a reason good enough."

Almost ten years have passed since we began our quest to understand suffering and the sovereignty of God. Ten years in which we struggled to find a reason for suffering. We believed then, although many of our beliefs were not logically coexistent, that God specifically chose certain people out to suffer, and that our good fortune was due to a "special blessing." We prayed for "protection" so that we could mystically escape the natural consequences of being human.

In those years, we watched our beautiful Punky regress from a healthy normal two-and-a-half year old, to a ten-year-old not even able to talk. We watched our son go through the hell of being burned. At least every other night for two years we were awake with him, as he attempted to run from the itchiness of his recovering burns. Indeed, it seemed as if he were trying to escape from out of his own skin. Those were nights we demanded our theology be logical and match with life as well as Scripture.

After several years of struggling with the the problem of suffering, we can see only one purpose to justify, not only our own suffering, but the "groaning of the creation" (Romans 8:18-25).

It is this: Suffering is a consequence of being *human.* Without choice, there is no humanity. Some of the strongest words of Christendom have become muddied and misunderstood with the passage of time. Words like "choice," and "free will". Although those were words I heard repeatedly while growing up to describe how one could know God, I received a mixed message. That was: "Free will is not really free. God purposes everything that happens—even the 'choices' you think you are making."

In his book, *Under the Mercy,* Sheldon Vanauken says:

> *Choice has consequences or it wouldn't be choice at all. If*
> *we pull the trigger, the bullet strikes, and our victim gasps*

and dies. If God gives us freedom, freedom to choose, He must allow us to have what we choose—the taste of the apple, the death of the man we shoot, or, if we insist, Hell— or it wouldn't be choice at all. He must allow the consequences, going on endlessly, involving the innocent. . . .

But there may be good consequences, too—God will bring these about if possible. You and your wife may learn to trust God more deeply; the young man, haunted by grief, may become a Christian. But those would be bringing good out of evil, not bringing evil in the hopes of the good. The evil was the consequences of a choice. To say that because God is sovereign and all powerful He can simultaneously give us freedom to choose and compel our choice is not to say something profound about omnipotence but to speak nonsense.

Vanauken, describing what would happen if God did "compel" the choices of mankind, adds:

Agony is not to be measured quantitatively. The 50 people in a gas chamber—a quick death, after all—or one man being hideously tortured, hour after hour, day after day, by the secret police. God stops that: no line can be drawn. And the woman in the hospital, her body eaten up by cancer: she is suffering almost as much or perhaps more—who can measure? God, committed now to action, acts. The woman draws a long breath, flinching. It doesn't hurt. She sits up and asks for lunch.

A rapist is leering down at his terrified victim. Then he finds an invisible wall between him and her. In a few moments she pulls her torn frock round her and goes, possibly sticking her tongue out at the shrunken man. . . . All this— it's right nice, isn't it? This is the God we want, we think. We are ready to reelect God, God. But let us look further . . . Finally it will dawn upon mankind that God has stopped all victimizing. You cannot shoot anybody, but also—since God can't draw lines—you cannot bark at your wife or cheat on your income tax. The fist cannot be clenched. The cruel word cannot be said. Free will has been repealed. No one now chooses to be good; he must be. *

*Vanauken, Sheldon, **Under the Mercy;** Thomas Nelson Publishers Nashville— Camden—New York, Copyright by Sheldon Vanauken, 1985, pp. 118-119, 120, 121. Used by permission.

As part of an intergenerational humanity, choices have been made that affect history. Choices beginning with Adam and Eve. Choices that bring the potential for art, music, sex, children, love, and murder, rape, incest, death, and autism.

God made us human; our humanity resulted in a fallen world. Perhaps, in that way, one could say God's "great purpose" is being fulfilled by the suffering of the world. The purpose, of having humans choose to love him and be loved by him of their own free will.

Understanding that it is God's plan to give humans free will, thereby denying Himself for a time some "control," doesn't seem a hopeless message to me. Our hope now rests in the ultimate redemption: Living in heaven, where Jeremy's scars will be no more, where his mind will be as perfect as anyone else's, where we will again hear him sing "Jesus Loves Me," where God will wipe all the tears from our eyes.

> *Dear Jeremy,*
> *Five years ago my joy knew no bounds.*
> *I was so proud of your dark hair, your blue eyes, your dainty features, and most of all your alertness.*
> *I knew then you were extra smart.*
> *(Why that has always been so important to me I still don't understand.)*
> *As you grew, we were more and more convinced of your unusual beauty, intelligence, and especially wonderful nature.*
> *And we were right . . . .*
> *But then, mysteriously it crept upon us, savagely wielding doubts into the beautiful future painted vividly in our minds.*
> *It took two years for us to realize that it wasn't just a minor learning disability.*
> *Over and over, hurt rears it's ugly head, bitter puss spewing from it.*
> *Our hurt is so intense for you, Jeremy. We long to talk to you to tell you how we feel, but we don't ever know if you hear us.*
> *Will we ever know?*
> *Jeremy. . . we cast aside our burden only when we see you for a moment, happy.*
> *We live for moments. We live from moment to moment . . . now.*
> *It is probably a better way to live.*
> *You though so little, so unlikely, have taught us already, so much!*

(Written on Jeremy's fifth birthday, Penny Giesbrecht, 1983)

Acknowledgements

When a Child Suffers is the product of many hearts and minds. Although I wrote the original draft it is only through the encouragement and support of friends and family that the book ever became a reality.

Dr. David Ahrenholz reviewed all of the chapters relating to Jeremy's burn injury both for medical accuracy and to provide the most recent information regarding burn prevention and treatment.

Sheldon Vanauken reviewed the Epilogue and graciously agreed to allow me to quote his most strategic thoughts about the free will of humankind.

Dr. Henry Panowitsch, Sheila Merzer, Lyle Chastain, Cindy Nollette, Dr. Carolyn Levitt, Rev. Mike Bortel, Neil & Shari Stavem, Darla & Steve Pesola, Al & Madge Leir, John & Marie Peterson, and Karen & Mark Baden willingly read the chapters of the manuscript relating to them. More importantly, they touched our lives with hope and strength in the time we needed it most.

Cyndy Johnson believed in the message of *When a Child Suffers* from the very beginning. In fact, she took Angele with her daughter Jennie to "Baby School" every Thursday morning for two years, leaving me with strict instructions: "Write!" I am indebted to her for tangibly showing her trust in my ability to record the beliefs we share about suffering and the sovereignty of God.

I called Candie and Drew Blankman long distance more than once to brainstorm with them about how God works in the world. Drew also provided as background material a research paper he'd written in seminary relating to suffering.

Three years ago I took a class called "Writing for Publication" at Northwestern College. Ruth Peterman, the instructor, became my writing workshop teacher, mentor, editor, and friend. I thank her for patiently teaching me the basics of writing and for providing me the forum to publicly state my beliefs about God's role in suffering.

Ultimately any book, no matter how many friends and family members think it's wonderful, needs a publisher. Without Jim and Marti Hefley's belief in the book it would still be only 400 K's of memory on my word processor. Thank you for your guidance, cooperative spirits, and patience as we "worked over" this manuscript again and again.

"Mommy, listen to me! You never listen when you're writing!" was a statement Charity or Angele made many times as I wrote and rewrote each chapter.

"Yell till I hear you if you really need me, and if you don't, go ask your father," was my standard reply.

When I started this book I wrote knowing the odds against its ever being published were high. Yet I had two reasons for recording these events. First, the details of the trauma were etched in my mind. I hoped that in writing it down catharsis would take place and I could let some of the pain go. Second, Jeremy's regression and burn injury have molded and shaped who I am. I was afraid to let my memories fade until they were safely on paper for my children and grandchildren. I wanted them to know why I am the person I am. They could never truly understand Tim or me without knowing about those early years that even Charity will never consciously remember. So thank you, kids, for being patient with your mom, because this book is for you.

The fact that the book is being published is the frosting on the cake. It is Tim's and my desire that the sharing of Jeremy's pain and our own struggle with suffering and the sovereignty of God will help many other fellow life strugglers.

Names and incidental details of a few people were changed to protect their privacy. We bear no grudges to those who said hurtful things to us. We are all only human beings struggling to understand ourselves, our place in the world, and our God.

In conclusion, I want to thank my best friend and the father of my three very lucky children, my husband Tim. It was through his encouragement that I pursued writing classes, workshops, and seminars. It was also through his belief in me that I had the courage to try to record these events. I am so thankful that Tim is my partner as we face life's struggles and joys together.

Penny Rosell Giesbrecht
761 Cottage Place
Shoreview, Minnesota
55126

Mail Coupon to:

Hannibal Books
31 Holiday Drive
Hannibal, MO 63401

Please send me copies

Where Is God When a Child Suffers?, by Penny
Rosell Giesbrecht

$8.95

**By Their Blood: Christian Martyrs of the 20th
Century**, by James and Marti Hefley. Winner of Gold
Medallion Award for "Best Christian Biography of Year"

$14.95

Way Back in the Hills, by James C. Hefley
Nostaligic true story of a boy growing up in a remote
Ozark valley during the 1930s and 1940s

$4.50

Life Changes, by James C. Hefley
For persons struggling through difficult life transitions

$5.95

Please add $1.25 postage and handling for first book, plus .50
each for additional books. Missouri residents add sales tax.

TOTAL ENCLOSED (check or money order) $ _____

Name _____

Address _____

City, State, Zip _____